I0621061

TWO TREES
ONE CHOICE

BY KIRSTEN DOUKAS

Copyright © 2025 by Kirsten Doukas. All Rights Reserved.

Unless otherwise indicated, all Scripture quotations are from The ESV® Bible (The Holy Bible, English Standard Version®), © 2001 by Crossway, a publishing ministry of Good News Publishers. Used by permission. All rights reserved.

Scripture quotations marked NLT are taken from the Holy Bible, New Living Translation, copyright ©1996, 2004, 2015 by Tyndale House Foundation. Used by permission of Tyndale House Publishers, Carol Stream, Illinois 60188. All rights reserved.

Cover and layout design by Kirsten Doukas, pastelblackdesign.com
Cover graphic compiled from photos by: Pixabay and Summer Stock
Headshot on back cover by Rachel Kemble

ISBN: 978-1-964959-99-3
eBook: 978-1-964959-98-6

This edition published by Seraph Creative in 2025
United States / United Kingdom / South Africa / Australia
www.seraphcreative.org

All rights reserved. No part of this book, artwork included, may be used or reproduced in any matter without the written permission of the publisher.

To the believer (or maybe-believer) who wants to know God beyond the limitations of an earth-based system and to break off the shackles of the system of sin, death and decay, this book is for you.

To my husband, Evan, without whom this book would not exist. It is very much a product of God's revelations to both of us, individually and collectively, as we have learned and grown together as one. Even on a practical level, this book would never have been written without your provision, love, and support. I love you!

TABLE OF CONTENTS

INTRODUCTION

God is a lover of the purest kind. He loves us with a wild, unbridled passion that we have difficulty understanding, and He longs for our love in return. God easily could have created us to be His love slaves, with no chance or choice of rejection. But love isn't love if it is forced. True love requires holding the object of affection with an open hand, knowing they might choose rejection and choose to walk away. God made us—in His image and likeness—to share with Him in His love and express that love to all creation.

We were created with the seeds of His characteristics embedded in every aspect of our being. Like Adam and Eve, we begin life as an immature expression of God's image and likeness. But God never intended that we stay in that immaturity, but rather that we grow into full maturity. Life on this earth is a gift with all its opportunities to learn and grow in that maturity. Life gives us time and space repeatedly to make the one choice that all choices ultimately boil down to: will we choose love or will we reject Him? (To choose love is to choose God, life and all things good.) The first choice to reject God was dramatic. But in subtle and blatant ways, we ultimately make the same choice Adam and Eve made a thousand times each day.

Eve was made in the image of God, yet she believed the lie that there was God-likeness that had been withheld from her, and that it was something she could obtain through her own striving, her own works.

In other words, she believed that she, in her own power, could earn the God-likeness that had already been given to her in its seed form. And by their own self-achieving efforts, taking and eating fruit that they were not yet mature enough to handle, in direct disobedience and ultimately rejection of God, Adam and Eve ushered into creation an entire system that was devoid of the characteristics of God, a system of self and striving that leads death in every way.

Today, we have constant opportunities to choose or reject love. To choose self is to reject love. God demonstrated His love in the life of Jesus. His love was devoid of self and striving, but instead put others before Himself. To love as Jesus loved is almost always the harder choice in life. To love is to let go of our own desires and needs and to prioritize what is best for others, unconditionally. To love unconditionally requires sacrifice, but it is a sacrifice that ultimately leads to true life.[1]

Love devoid of self and striving is the only path to life. But love devoid of striving is not devoid of action. Love is action. And love is surrender to the One who is love itself.

Who wouldn't want to go back to the beginning, to the garden in Eden and see what it was like, to walk with God in the cool of the day, and to experience life before the fall, before evil corrupted the world and the hearts of humanity? What was it like for Adam and Eve? Can we ever get back to that place, or is the world doomed forever?

---

1   "Whoever finds his life will lose it, and whoever loses his life for my sake will find it." (Matthew 10:39)

Thankfully, God was not surprised by the self-serving, destructive actions of Adam and Eve. The Bible says that Jesus was known[2] and slain[3] before the foundation of the world. He became a second Adam[4] (a second chance for humanity), defeated sin and death,[5] and restored humanity back to the Father!

Yet, if we are honest, we do not see all of the promises of restoration yet manifested around us. Why do we still experience death in its many forms (physical, spiritual, mental, emotional, financial, relational, etc.) in our lives if Jesus defeated death? The answer to that is not an easy one and would take volumes to unpack, and this book certainly does not address everything. On a universal scale, we wait eagerly alongside all creation for the Sons of God and the promises of life to be revealed.[6] But on an individual scale, I believe there are reasons we do not yet see life and its promises manifest.

Often in life in this world, surrounded by a system of self-serving manifestations of the absence of God, it is difficult to understand the true nature of God, and therefore, His true intent for us and our lives. We may have heard and even believe that God is loving and that He ran-

---

2   "He was foreknown before the foundation of the world but was made manifest in the last times for the sake of you who through him are believers in God, who raised him from the dead and gave him glory, so that your faith and hope are in God." (1 Peter 1:20-21)

3   "...the Lamb who was slaughtered before the world was made." (Revelation 13:8b)

4   1 Corinthians 15:45-49

5   "'O death, where is your victory? O death, where is your sting?' The sting of death is sin, and the power of sin is the law. But thanks be to God, who gives us the victory through our Lord Jesus Christ." (1 Corinthians 15:55-57)

6   Romans 8:18-23

somed us back to right standing with Him, yet we live as though we have to do something to earn that love and position with Him when it has already been freely given. We may say we believe in Jesus and the finished work of the cross, yet we live as though our works somehow add to what He did. Ultimately, we sometimes still live selfishly and love like the world loves. How we live reveals what we truly believe, and what we believe manifests powerfully in how we live.

To put it another way, the Tree of Life and the Tree of the Knowledge of Good and Evil are alive and well today, producing and reproducing in every aspect of our lives and in every choice we make. Consciously and unconsciously, we perpetuate the same mistakes that Adam and Eve made in their self-centered disobedience and rejection of God, and we mistakenly apply the self-centered system of death and separation onto our image of God and therefore onto ourselves. We must learn to separate our own ideas of self-made works and striving from the true nature of God and learn to accept His unconditional love. We must learn to live a life of surrender to Him, to learn to work from a place of rest, knowing He has already done it all, and that our job is merely to manifest Him and His love in all creation.

I invite you to set aside what you think you believe for a moment and consider the possibility that there is more to the story than we previously have understood. Beliefs matter. This book attempts to address a few of those beliefs that may be tying you to a self-made system of fear and death and hindering you from living the fullness of life that has been given to us through Jesus.

CHAPTER 1
THE CHOICE

In the beginning (of what we call the beginning), God created the universe, and everything in it. God, in His infinite wisdom, and out of a desire for family, created people in His likeness and image. (Before us, He created many heavenly beings, but we are unique in that we are made *like* Him.) He breathed His own breath of life into them, male and female, two parts of a single whole, and created them from the very blueprint of God Himself. In many ways, they were like infants, *like* their Father in every way, yet lacking in knowledge, understanding and maturity. They walked with God and talked with Him. But in their childlike innocence, like an infant who knows nothing but the simplest needs of life and a desire for the closeness of mother, they knew nothing about right and wrong, good or evil.

Were they literally infants? Likely not, since they could walk and talk and were expected to tend to the garden and animals. But were they walking in the fullness of the maturity of their created likeness? Definitely not, as we will see shortly.

God placed them, Adam and Eve, the first people, in a garden of delight, called Eden. (The word *Eden* literally means *delight*.) He planted trees in the garden for food and for enjoyment. Out of all the trees in the garden, there were two that were particularly noteworthy. The first was the Tree of Life, whose fruit allowed life eternal when eaten. The second was called the Tree of the Knowledge of Good and Evil, whose fruit ultimately would bring death, not just to those who ate it, but to the entirety of this new creation, as we will find out later in the story. God gave them permission to eat of any tree in the garden, except for the second tree (which I will call the *Tree of Knowledge* for short).

GOD, AND ALL HE MADE, IS GOOD

In the beginning, God created, and it was *good*.[1] All of it. He called it so, and God cannot lie.[2] "All things were made through him, and without him was not any thing made that was made." (John 1:3) That would imply that even the Tree of Knowledge was created by God Himself. If God is a good God,[3] as the Bible repeatedly tells us He is, how could He create something that could, and has, produced such evil? The answer, surprisingly, is found in love.[4] But if God *is* love[5] and God *is* good, how can love Himself even *allow* the possibility of evil to exist, never mind create and allow access to it?

---

1   "For everything created by God is good, and nothing is to be rejected if it is received with thanksgiving..." (1 Timothy 4:4)

2   "...it is impossible for God to lie..." (Hebrews 6:18b)

3   "Oh give thanks to the Lord, for he is good; for his steadfast love endures forever!" (1 Chronicles 16:34)

4   When I say "love," I am referring to the self-sacrificial love of God Himself, as modeled to us by Jesus Christ, and not the self-serving and often destructive "love" of the world, which we will get into later.

5   "So we have come to know and to believe the love that God has for us. God is love, and whoever abides in love abides in God, and God abides in him." (1 John 4:16)

Think about it this way: God easily could have created robotic creatures who had no other option than to love Him. But is that truly love if it is compulsory and there is no other option? I believe that it would go against the very nature of God Himself to create a love-slave who is unable to choose. God is not a self-serving being, and rather would give everything for those He loves, as demonstrated by Jesus Himself.[6] A love that is *required* by others is self-serving and would be merely servitude at best and slavery at worst. That kind of "love" is not love at all and is contrary to the very self-sacrificial nature of God, who would give up everything to restore us back into right-standing relationship with Him. Mandatory love is the abusive type of "love" too often demonstrated in the world. *That* sounds evil to me. Even if God *could* make love mandatory, how gratifying would that be to God, wanting to be loved, and only being loved because the creature He made had no other choice? God, in His infinite wisdom, *knows* that true love, like His own love, is self-sacrificial and *has* to come with the option of choice, otherwise it is not love at all.

God is in everything, everywhere,[7] and there is nowhere that He is not.[8] If He saturates everything, and if His being is so awesome and glorious, the very essence of love and goodness itself, how could anyone choose anything *but* to love Him? Unless at times, and in places, He makes Himself so small, so imperceptible that we are provided the illu-

---

6   "In this the love of God was made manifest among us, that God sent his only Son into the world, so that we might live through him." (1 John 4:9)

7   "...one God and Father of all, who is over all and through all and in all." (Ephesians 4:6)

8   "If I ascend to heaven, you are there! If I make my bed in Sheol, you are there!" (Psalm 139:8)

sion of separation and distance by which to choose Him willingly. We must seek Him out of desire, out of the longing for Him created by the perception of separation. Like a loving Daddy, playing hide-and-seek with a beloved toddler, He hides Himself in plain sight, purely for the joy of being found.

To choose to love God is to choose God Himself (and conversely, to reject God's love is to reject God Himself). In order for a creature to be able to choose God or not, there had to be something other than God. However, God did not create a substance or force in contrast to Himself, He merely created pockets of the absence of Himself, a void devoid of Himself. In other words, He did not create an entity called Evil, rather evil is merely the expression of the absence of God. Evil is simply anything that is not like God and is devoid of God. So, we are now given a choice to either choose God actively, or actively (and sometimes unintentionally) turn our backs away from Him and toward the absence of Him (the absence itself being evil). The action itself of turning away from God toward evil is evil and is also known as sin. And we become what we face, what we behold,[9] whether good or evil.

Choose wisely.

---

9 "And we all, with unveiled face, beholding the glory of the Lord, are being transformed into the same image from one degree of glory to another. For this comes from the Lord who is the Spirit." (2 Corinthians 3:18)

"And those who make idols are just like them, as are all who trust in them." (Psalm 115:8 NLT)

CHAPTER 2
DECEPTION AND DISOBEDIENCE

Adam (and later, Eve) was placed in the garden that God planted in Eden.[1] Adam was given the job of tending and caring for the garden.[2] God gave Adam the fruit of every tree of the garden to eat, except for the Tree of the Knowledge of Good and Evil, and told him, "for in the day that you eat of it, you shall surely die."[3]

God gave them many options of good fruit to eat, and only one of the trees was off-limits. Ultimately, God gave them many choices to obey Him, and only one choice to disobey. God loves us with the essence of *who He is* more profoundly than we can imagine, so He would never, could never, tell us to do anything that would separate us from Him; if He tells us to do something, it is with ultimate good in mind. God cannot command us to do something that is contrary to His nature. To do so would be evil, which is the absence of everything He is. To

---

1 "And the Lord God planted a garden in Eden, in the east, and there he put the man whom he had formed." (Genesis 2:8)

2 "The Lord God took the man and put him in the garden of Eden to work it and keep it." (Genesis 2:15)

3 "And the Lord God commanded the man, saying, 'You may surely eat of every tree of the garden, but of the tree of the knowledge of good and evil you shall not eat, for in the day that you eat of it you shall surely die.'" (Genesis 2:16-17)

obey God is to choose God and to choose everything that is God. To disobey God is to choose everything that God is not. We are accustomed to people walking in evil (the absence of God) and commanding obedience to themselves out of a place of evil, so we tend to think very scornfully of the idea of obedience, but forced obedience to evil is contrary to God and everything He wishes for creation. God is looking for willing obedience for our own good. When we choose obedience to God, we step out of the absence of Him and into the presence of Him and everything that He is. Remember that God's desire from the beginning is that we choose to love Him, and when we do, we receive all the blessings contained in Him.

Side note: The world has a very twisted idea of who God is, mostly because the gods of this world are fallen, self-serving beings, who have chosen to turn their backs on the true God, and therefore exhibit all the features of who God is not: evil. The idea of who God is also becomes further muddled and abused as evil people seek their own power through the twisting and perverting of religious systems (including organizations that began with the good intent to draw people toward the one true God). This is where the Bible becomes invaluable, and a genuine pursuit of relationship with the person of God Himself is irreplaceable. You can learn about Him by reading about Him and talking to others about him, but to *truly know Him,* you must get to know Him personally, as you would any other being: talk to Him, listen to Him, and yes, learn from others about Him. The idea of the nature of *who God is* could easily take up many, many volumes of writing. For the sake of this book, when I say that God is good, that includes all things truly good, such as "love, joy, peace, patience, kindness, goodness, faithfulness, gentleness, self-control,"[4] and so much more.

We don't know how long Adam and Eve were in the garden, but they walked with God and talked with Him, and they ate from the fruit of the trees in the garden. (I do wonder what other trees were planted in that garden and if the Tree of Life was the most prominent among them. Were there merely fig and apple trees? Or perhaps, were there trees of Joy and Wisdom?)

We do know that alongside this garden and this new creation, there was a non-physical realm of beings including angels—including the gods of this world mentioned before—whom had also been given the choice to obey and choose God, but chose instead to promote themselves at the cost of separating themselves away from God, and into all things evil, aka. not like God. These now-self-serving beings wanted to be like God, but without the Source of good Himself, and through their freedom to choose, they chose the absence of life and became slaves to death, spreading death, lies and destruction everywhere they went, including in the garden in Eden. They hated the new children of God, knowing that no matter what they did, they could never actually truly be God Himself, and they *hated* Him for it. But these new creatures God made, humans, were just like Him. And they *hated* them for it. So, what better way to hurt the God they could never be like than to destroy the creatures that He made to be just like Himself?

---

4   "But the fruit of the Spirit is love, joy, peace, patience, kindness, goodness, faithfulness, gentleness, self-control; against such things there is no law." (Galatians 5:22-23)

EVIL DECEIVES

Enter deception, in the form of a serpent. Metaphorically speaking, serpents are evil in physical form, lying, deceiving, and generally toxic. Ancient peoples would have read the creation story and would have understood that this was not just an ordinary animal, but rather the manifestation of one of the fallen spiritual beings, one of the heavenly beings who had chosen to exalt himself to a self-serving position as a god of this world. John, in the book of Revelation, further identifies this "serpent" as the devil, also known as Satan (which is a title that means *the accuser*).[5]

Satan comes to Eve, and offers her several lies, causing her to doubt. He says, "Did God actually say, 'You shall not eat of any tree in the garden?'"[6] As in, is God withholding good things from you? Is God really good? Does God really want you to be happy? *Does God really love you?* These are still among the most prominent lies of the enemy in our lives today.

Eve responds with, "We may eat of the fruit of the trees in the garden, but God said, 'You shall not eat of the fruit of the tree that is in the midst of the garden, neither shall you touch it, lest you die.'"[7] (I do wonder if Adam told Eve not to even touch it, adding to God's original

---

5   "And he seized the dragon, that ancient serpent, who is the devil and Satan, and bound him for a thousand years..." (Revelation 20:2)

6   Genesis 3:1b

7   Genesis 2:2b-3

instructions, perhaps out of a desire to protect her? Or perhaps she just added that part herself?)

"But the serpent said to the woman, 'You will not surely die. For God knows that when you eat of it your eyes will be opened, and you will be like God, knowing good and evil.'"[8] The interesting thing here is that Satan would have known that she was already made like God. Eve should have known that she was made like God. But his challenging of her identity caused her to doubt herself and her identity. (This is another of the enemy's primary tactics with us today.) There was a little bit of truth to his question, as there is a little bit of truth in any believable lie: Eve, in her innocence and lack of fullness of maturity, did not know the difference between good and evil. (If she had already known it, there would have been no temptation.) She fell for the lie, hook, line, and sinker. If she did not know good and evil like God, then it must be true: she must not be like God. Rather than believing what God said about her, that she was made like Him, she took matters into her own hands, and out of her own means and abilities, tried to make herself like God in her own power, instead of just receiving the gift of her identity from the creator Himself. And in so doing, she disobeyed God, and like the fallen being in front of her, chose evil and the absence of God Himself.

---

8   Genesis 4-5

SIN REPRODUCES

The interesting thing about fruit is that it always replicates after its own kind. A pear tree produces pears, which contain pear seeds, which produce pear trees. Jesus said that you can know what kind of a tree something is by the type of fruit that is produced.[9] As soon as Eve ate the fruit, its seed began to replicate in her, as the seeds of any tree do, and more trees were planted. In other words, fear was planted in her, and the first thing Eve did was to give some of the fruit to her husband, Adam. He ate as well, planting fear and death in him as well.

1 Timothy 2:14 says that "Adam was not deceived." That is a loaded statement! Eve was deceived, but Adam chose to disobey intentionally. Someday, I would love to know the reason why he did what he did, and we could speculate endlessly about that now, but in the end, we would only be left with speculation. All we know are the facts: Eve was deceived, Adam was not. Regardless, they both ate. They both disobeyed. They both turned their backs on God and stepped outside of everything that He is, turning their faces toward everything that God is not.

We usually think of sin as something we have done wrong, which is only a part of the picture. Sin is the action of disobeying what God says is good to do. What He says is good is everything that He is; therefore, the action of sin is an active turning of our backs on God. Sin then becomes a position, a state of being, and sin is everything that is not like God.

---

9 "Either make the tree good and its fruit good, or make the tree bad and its fruit bad, for the tree is known by its fruit..." (Matthew 12:33)

THE JUDGEMENT OF ONE WHO KNOWS GOOD AND EVIL

Before Adam ate, he did not know the difference between right and wrong, good and evil; but he did know what it meant to obey. If you have ever observed a dog with its master, you will know that the dog really does not understand that stealing its master's food is wrong or evil, but rather that the dog just knows that if it is caught, its master will be angry. Adam had to have known that God would be heartbroken by his disobedience. But he chose to disobey anyway, whatever his reasons. And as soon as he ate, he *knew* what he had done was wrong.

One of God's attributes is that of Judge, and Adam and Eve were also made with that attribute. Adam judged himself, correctly, as one guilty of disobedience, and worthy of death, which is separation from God. Separation from God was Adam's judgment, not God's. (Remember: God came looking for Adam and Eve, as they ran and hid from Him.) God removed Adam and Eve from the garden of Eden to protect them from eating of the Tree of Life and living forever as dead, but God did not remove them from His presence. Rather, shortly after, we see God outside the garden as well, talking with Cain. In other words, even though Adam and Eve separated themselves from God's presence, God never stopped pursuing them or their children.

The serpent was right, in a way, about one thing. They didn't die that day, at least not *physically*. That was a part of the deception. But when Adam *knew* what he had done, he understood that choosing against God meant choosing death, and he judged himself guilty and worthy of that death.[10] On that day they did die, spiritually, and that spiritual death did not just stay with them, it spread to all of Creation around them, as that fruit of death began to spread its seed into all Creation.

The choice they made, and the choice we make daily, is really a choice of life and death. Do we choose life Himself, or do we choose death without Him. Every choice we make in life comes down to this. The choice is ultimately not about right and wrong, good and evil; the understanding of both those things is found in the Tree of Knowledge, and the fruit of that tree is death. (You will know a tree by its fruit!) The real choice is between two trees: the Tree of Life and the Tree of Death. *Spoiler alert:* if we fast-forward the story several thousand years, Jesus, as God's representative in physical form on Earth, is offered to us as the Tree of Life, and by choosing Him, eating from the fruit of His life, [11] we actively choose life Himself.

---

10   How often do we as believers judge ourselves guilty, and technically we are right, yet the blood of Jesus has already cleansed us, forgiven us, from that guilt? He is no longer looking on our sin the way we do.

11   "'I am the living bread that came down from heaven. If anyone eats of this bread, he will live forever. And the bread that I will give for the life of the world is my flesh.'" (John 6:51)

CHAPTER 3
RIGHT AND WRONG ACCORDING TO WHOM?

You might be wondering, "Was the Tree of Knowledge a necessary evil, then?" (*Necessary*, as in providing a choice, and *evil* for its ability to allow us to choose something other than God and Godlikeness.) Yes, in the way that we needed a way to choose to love God or not. But really, no, in the way that the question itself actually leads us into misunderstanding God, because it is so wrapped up in our limited understanding and experience as humans, with our thinking enshrined in the good versus evil paradigm, established through the Tree of Knowledge. We must elevate our thinking above simple good versus evil in order to understand God's higher reality and understanding, which is love.

As I mentioned before, the Tree of Knowledge was included among all God created and was not excluded from all that God called good. (It is the Tree of the Knowledge of *Good* and Evil, after all.) God is everywhere, and there is nowhere He is not, which means there is nowhere that is not full of His goodness; yet God made a void of Himself in order to allow a choice of something other than Himself. So, if God cannot *create* evil, but only make a void within Himself of the absence of Himself (and all the things He is), how can He *create* a tree with the fruit of death? If He cannot create evil, and He called the Tree good, and if God cannot lie, then the Tree of Knowledge *must* be inherently good. God called the Tree good, so it is, by definition, not evil. So, it is not the tree itself that is the problem, but rather something else.

We have two major things at play here. The first being, the *disobedience* by Adam and Eve (where the choice to turn away from God is entwined). The disobedience, and following judgment of guilt, is what caused the separation from God. Remember, to obey God is to choose to participate in everything that He is: life, goodness, love, peace, patience, joy, wisdom, etc. To choose to disobey God is to position ourselves outside of Him, causing us to experience everything that He is not: death, hate, fear, isolation, foolishness, selfishness, and so many other negatives. Those are among the fruits of disobedience. We also experience those negatives as a result of living in a fallen world; we experience our own deathlike choices and the natural consequence of being surrounded by others who are also manifesting a lack of God and sowing seeds of death all around them. When we disobey, we position ourselves in death and the very lack of God and all He is. When we obey God, we position ourselves to receive and live in the blessing of all that He is.

In essence, evil (and all it encompasses) is actually a natural consequence of separation from good rather than a created entity, characteristic, or even punishment. If a man stands in the warmth of a fire, he will be warm. If he leaves the house and goes out into the cold, he will no longer feel the warmth of the fire or experience its benefit. The fire does not punish the man for leaving by removing its blessing or inflicting cold; the cold is merely a byproduct of the absence of the fire and a natural consequence of the man's choice to leave the house. This metaphor of the fire is extremely limited in comparison to the goodness of God, but hopefully, you get the idea. Evil is a lack of the goodness of God just as darkness is an absence of light.

The second major thing at play is the gaining of *knowledge* of the difference between good and evil. The Tree is not called the Tree of Good and Evil. It is the Tree of the *Knowledge* of Good and Evil. Animals do not understand the difference between good and evil. A bird is not wrong for stealing a gardener's fruit. A lion is not wrong for killing a zebra. They do not know the difference between right and wrong, and merely act according to their nature (fallen though it might be at the moment). Adam and Eve ate the fruit of the Tree of the Knowledge of Good and Evil, and in an instant understood that some things were right and others were wrong, and as a consequence gained the ability to judge accordingly. That ability to know right from wrong, and to judge accordingly, has been passed down to all of humanity.

HUMANITY AS JUDGE

What is interesting about our ability to judge right from wrong is that we will judge according to where we are positioned: in God, or out of God. Adam and Eve, because of their choice to disobey, were positioned outside of God, separate from Him, and they began to judge according to their position outside of God. Likewise, our judgments will be based on our perception and beliefs, according to the fruit of evil, and our position in the lack of God (the lack of goodness and the presence of God). We remain positioned outside of God until we repent, turn our back on sin and all that God is not, and receive the free gift of forgiveness offered to us by Jesus.

When Adam and Eve disobeyed God, the fallen, earth-based system that we are born into was formed. When they chose to follow the Deceiver, they were obedient to his voice, and therefore positioned themselves under his government and lordship, making him the god over them, while simultaneously removing themselves from the government and Lordship of the one true God. The Deceiver had already established himself by his own disobedience as separate from God, making himself a god over the void of God: god of the absence of life, love and all that is good. And now, with the deception and betrayal of Adam and Eve, he had successfully made subjects and slaves of the very children of his mortal enemy, the One True God. And all of creation fell with them and became subject to bondage in this new earth-based system.

RIGHT AND WRONG ACCORDING TO WHOM?

For thousands of years, the children of Adam and Eve knew nothing but right and wrong as they saw it and judged it. The Bible says that in those days, "everyone did what was right in his own eyes."[1] What that means is that they did what *they* judged to be right, according to their own perspective, in their position contrary to the ways of God. It wasn't

---

1   Judges 17:6b

for thousands of years, until the Law[2] was given to Moses, that God began to teach His children how *He* judges right and wrong, good and evil. Much of this instruction was done by revealing Himself and His attributes to His people, and He revealed Himself through His laws. Once more, the people of Israel were given the choice to obey God and live in His blessings, or disobey and live cursed, outside of God's blessings. Once more, humanity was invited into relationship with their creator.

For the people of Israel, the Law of Moses served as a tutor and guide, drawing them back to the heart of their true Father.[3] The people were still positioned outside of God, in sin; they still carried the record of disobedience, the fruit of the Tree of Knowledge. But through the covering of the blood of animal sacrifices and through obedience to the Law, they were able to come into a covenantal relationship and learn what it looks like to live *in* the presence and fullness of God. And they were given the promise of a Messiah who would come and make all things right, who would not just *cover* sin, but *remove* it, and wash it clean permanently, allowing people to return once again to right-standing in the presence of God and His goodness.

As we read through the history of the people of Israel in the Old Covenant, we read so many accounts of people who chose not to obey, and

---

2   Throughout this book the word "law" will be capitalized when referring explicitly to the Law of Moses.

3   "But before faith came, we were kept under guard by the law, kept for the faith which would afterward be revealed. Therefore the law was our tutor to bring us to Christ, that we might be justified by faith." (Galatians 3:23-24)

"did what was right in their own eyes,"[4] even with God's example of what He says is right and wrong in front of them. But there are the gems who chose to follow God, and it is often noted that a specific person "did what was right in the eyes of the Lord,"[5] sometimes half-heartedly, sometimes wholeheartedly. Often, it is specifically noted that it was done in the way shown to him by his father, or in the way demonstrated by a prominent figure like King David.

An infant does not understand that breaking someone else's things is wrong, but a teenager who has been taught manners and morals should know that it is wrong. With growth and worldly instruction, we all gain the understanding of good and evil, and we judge according to worldly systems and our position outside of God. With maturity and Godly instruction, we begin to learn how God sees good and evil. If we are wise and choose to turn to Him and follow His ways, we can then judge and live accordingly, reaping the benefits of our inclusion in God. Or, if we turn away from Him, we reap the curses of our own self-imposed exclusion. We are all offered the same choice that Adam and Eve were offered, to choose God or to turn away from Him. It is not a choice of which tree to eat from physically, but it is the same choice, nonetheless.

---

4   "In those days there was no king in Israel. Everyone did what was right in his own eyes." (Judges 21:25)

5   See: 2 Chronicles 14:2; 2 Chronicles 25:2; 1 Kings 15:11; 2 Chronicles 24:2; 2 Chronicles 29:2; etc.

CHAPTER 4
MATURITY

Consider this: Adam and Eve learned the difference between right and wrong, and it produced death in them; God Himself knows the difference between good and evil, and yet this knowledge does *not* produce death in Him. How is that possible? The answer is found in who God is, and His self-sacrificial love as manifest in the example of the life lived by Jesus on this earth.

God knew the difference between good and evil, and He must have created Adam and Eve without this ability for a reason. As I have said before, knowing the difference between good and evil would have been desirable to Eve only if she did not already have the ability. He also provided a way through which to gain this ability, this knowing, through the creation of the Tree of Knowledge, yet he made the tree off-limits. Why? This was the one command that God gave to Adam and Eve prior to their fall: do not eat of the Tree of the Knowledge of Good and Evil.[1] Assuming this was the only commandment given prior to the fall, this was the *only* way for Adam and Eve to disobey God. There must have been hundreds or thousands of other trees that

---

1 "And the Lord God commanded the man, saying, "You may surely eat of every tree of the garden, but of the tree of the knowledge of good and evil you shall not eat, for in the day that you eat of it you shall surely die." (Genesis 2:16-17)

were totally permissible, and only one that was off-limits. Hundreds and thousands of blessings, but only one potential for failure.

The tree itself was good. The knowledge it contained did not have a deathlike effect on the God who created it. God could have given them the commandment not to eat of the tree merely for the purpose of providing a choice of something other than Himself, a choice to obey or disobey.[2] They had to have some kind of choice, otherwise they would not have been able to freely choose relationship with God, so an arbitrary choice would technically be sufficient.

I believe there is more to God's intentional omission of the knowledge of good and evil in the creation of Adam and Eve, and that answer lies in maturity, and specifically the understanding that comes with maturity. Even more specifically, maturity as defined by the nature and likeness of God. Adam and Eve may or may not have been created as infants, but I believe their immaturity made it so that they could not handle the knowledge of good and evil without that knowledge having a corrupting, deadly effect. Yes, it was their disobedience that positioned Adam and Eve outside of life in God, causing effective death, but in their lack of God's maturity, they also lacked an extremely im-

---

2 We have the opportunity to obey or disobey God daily, moment to moment. Our choices have consequences, good or bad, just as there were consequences for Adam and Eve's disobedience. Thankfully, our choices usually do not come with consequences as severe as what Adam and Eve experienced. Our obedience (or lack thereof) positions ourselves inside or outside of the blessings of God. However, because of the new covenant established by the blood of Jesus, it is not our *obedience* that qualifies us for salvation and position with or without God, but rather it is our *belief* in Jesus that allows us to receive salvation and inherit His right-standing and inclusion in God. Our obedience will very much affect our daily lives and the lives of everyone around us, for good or bad, but because of the self-sacrificial love of Jesus, those consequences do not have to be permanent.

portant characteristic: the fullness of God's understanding of the self-sacrificial nature of love as defined by God Himself. More simply, they lacked understanding and experience of how God loves. God would have known the detrimental effect this knowledge of good and evil would have had on someone who does not yet fully know and understand His true, self-sacrificial love. I believe He placed restrictions on the Tree of Knowledge in order to protect them from premature exposure and its consequential harm.

Another way to say it is that true understanding of God's love and its self-sacrificial nature brings a maturity that enables one to know the difference between good and evil, without that knowledge having deadly effect.

SELF-FOCUSED "LOVE" PRODUCES DEATH

As humans on this earth, we often think of love as defined by the "what's in it for me?" kind of self-serving "love" that permeates societies and cultures around the globe. It is a false love based on emotion that comes and goes with self-serving desire, a love that takes first and gives only when it benefits the giver. That kind of "love" is conditional upon the benefit (or potential benefit) to the "lover." It comes and goes like the wind, and at its worst, leaves behind chaos, destruction, and death. It is the kind of "love" that seems right to a person who is living apart from God and exhibiting all the signs and symptoms of that separation. It is selfishness and self-centeredness masquerading as love.

When Eve took and ate the fruit, it was out of a selfish desire for what she could get for herself, by her own effort, without regard to how it would affect anyone or anything else. She was deceived and may not have fully understood what the consequences of her own actions would be. She likely did not understand what death really meant, either, living in a world where nothing had ever died before. Selfish desire is often like that, promising satisfaction and reward, with little thought or understanding of potential negative consequences for self or others, often in immature ignorance. And that same self-seeking, self-serving desire absolutely permeates every aspect of the fallen nature of humanity and the world around us.

THE LAW OF MOSES AND THE TREE OF THE KNOWLEDGE OF GOOD AND EVIL

Even the Law of Moses, with all its signposts pointing to the nature of God, with all its revelation on how to live as one separate from the fallen nature of the world, still operated under the system of right and wrong, good and evil. The apostle Paul referred to it as "the law of sin and death"[3] because it was a legal system established within the confines of the consequences of the Tree of Knowledge which says that when we are in sin, we experience death. It was a far better system of right and wrong than any other system in the rest of the world at the time, as it revealed instructions on how to live according to what God says is right and wrong, thereby giving the people who followed access

---

3   "For the law of the Spirit of life has set you free in Christ Jesus from the law of sin and death." (Romans 8:2)

to God's blessings. It was necessary and life-giving in an otherwise evil world. It was absolutely a *HUGE* leap in the right direction. But ultimately, it was still operational within the self-driven system of right and wrong, good and evil. At that point in history, immediately following 400 years of slavery to the Egyptians, law was all the people of Israel could accept, because of the harshness of their slavery[4] to the fear of death.[5] They did not have the capacity to accept an unearned gift of grace through relationship with God. The law-based system they could accept was a self-driven system of performance: what can I do or not do in order to bring myself back into relationship with God? It was a good start (at least they were heading toward God...sometimes), but it was not the final promise. They knew through God's prophets that when Messiah would come, He would bring about an even better way, a better system, and He did, in every way!

SELFLESS LOVE PRODUCES LIFE

Jesus was, and is, our signpost, pointing the way back to our creator, revealing His nature through every thought, word, and action. He is our example of a true, God-like love and our example of how to live. He did not live for what He could *get* from others and from life, but rather from what He could *give* to others, and he gave everything, including

---

4   "Moses spoke thus to the people of Israel, but they did not listen to Moses, because of their broken spirit and harsh slavery." (Exodus 6:9)

5   "Since therefore the children share in flesh and blood, he himself likewise partook of the same things, that through death he might destroy the one who has the power of death, that is, the devil, and deliver all those who through fear of death were subject to lifelong slavery." (Hebrews 2: 14-15)

even his very life. He demonstrated the love of the good Father, a love that gives and expects nothing in return, a love that sees only the value of being a created child of God and overlooks manmade societal constructs, a love that puts others first, a truly selfless love. It is that kind of love that every person needs and longs for more deeply than anything else, and it is that kind of love that rocked the world then and now. If only one person wholly living God's love could change the world so profoundly as Jesus' love did, imagine if all who believed in Jesus would learn to love like that! How the world would change!

Jesus had every opportunity to choose just as we all do, yet He was given a clean slate for choice. He was able to choose freely and without the record of sin and death from the Tree of Knowledge and the influence of fear (just as Adam chose freely), because He was born not of an earthly father, but rather conceived by the Holy Spirit. This is why Jesus is referred to as the second Adam. He was the second chance for humanity. The seed of the Tree of Knowledge had been planted in every descendant of Adam, along with its slavery to the fear of death. Jesus was given a tremendous gift to be born without that seed of death, and the freedom of choice that came with it, but oh, how great was the responsibility and sacrifice, and how great is His reward!

Jesus was tempted in every way that we are tempted,[6] yet He chose always to obey God and follow His commandments. He knew His heavenly Father intimately and stayed in constant communication and relationship with Him. Even though He was born without the seed of

---

6 "For we do not have a high priest who is unable to sympathize with our weaknesses, but one who in every respect has been tempted as we are, yet without sin." (Hebrews 4:15)

the Tree of Knowledge, He had earthly parents who taught Him good and evil according to God's standards as presented through the Law of Moses. There is also the possibility that God granted Jesus the full knowledge of good and evil at an early age, along with the fullness of understanding of self-sacrificial love that comes with maturity in God. Either way, Jesus was without sin his entire life, which means not once did He disobey God, not once did He act outside of the nature and character of God, His heavenly Father. He could have disobeyed at any moment, but he chose not to.

Jesus said He could not do anything except exactly as He saw the Father doing it.[7] I believe that Jesus' love for the Father and love for others compelled Him to only obey everything He was asked to do. Could He have chosen disobedience according to His own desires? Absolutely! He had every temptation to do so, yet because He truly *knew* the Father, and *understood* His love, disobedience wasn't an option. He lived a life *fully* obedient to God in every way, and because of that, He fully abided in God in every way, and fully expressed God's nature in every way. Jesus is our example of a *mature* son of God.

---

7   "So Jesus said to them, "Truly, truly, I say to you, the Son can do nothing of his own accord, but only what he sees the Father doing. For whatever the Father does, that the Son does likewise. For the Father loves the Son and shows him all that he himself is doing. And greater works than these will he show him, so that you may marvel." (John 5:19-20)

CHAPTER 5
FRUIT

Through this book so far, we have been discussing the fruit of the two focal-point trees in the garden of Eden. Not once have I mentioned what kind of fruit we are talking about physically (was it an apple tree, or maybe it was a fig tree, or maybe an olive tree?), and that is intentional, as discussed in the Introduction of this book. I believe we lose much of the meaning of Scripture when we choose to look only at its literal understanding, especially when that is not how the original readers would have understood the text. I want to continue in this vein and discuss the metaphorical nature of trees and fruit, particularly in its application to our daily lives.

So far, we have been talking almost exclusively in this book about two trees, the Tree of the Knowledge of Good and Evil and the Tree of Life. I believe neither are currently growing on this earth, at least not in the way that pear and walnut trees grow. The two trees may have been physical trees in the Garden of Eden, but for the focus of this book, I would like to look entirely at the non-physical manifestations of the trees. Primarily, I want to propose that the fruit of those two original trees are still reproducing constantly in every one of us.

The primary purpose of fruit is reproduction. A tree yields fruit that carries a seed (or many seeds), which when planted, produces more of that same tree, which produces more fruit, more seeds, more trees, and on and on. Eventually, with good soil, adequate water and sun, and the right climate, it is possible to plant an entire forest of the same kind of tree. Conditions can be such that this process can be hindered or stopped altogether, but that is the intended, natural process: reproduction.

In biblical times, nearly every person was engaged in agricultural production of some kind, or at the very least, was aware of the process of food production, including fruit production. Agricultural metaphors are used constantly throughout Scripture, particularly since it is a primary way that God speaks to us and shows us His nature, and it is how the original writers and readers would have understood Him best. It is a concept that would have been highly understandable to most cultures throughout history. We have become a little out of touch in our modern era of grocery stores and their conveniences. However, this is a simple enough concept to observe even in a modern city-dweller's life, with a little effort.

Jesus spoke to His broader audiences primarily in parables (metaphor-laced stories that reveal layers of truth and the potential for life-changing application). Many of His parables revolved around agriculture. One such parable talks about fruit and seed, such as we have been discussing in this book so far:

> *"For no good tree bears bad fruit, nor again does a bad tree bear good fruit, each tree is known by its own fruit. For figs are not gathered from thornbushes, nor are grapes picked from a bramble bush. The good person out of the good treasure of his heart produces good, and the evil person out of his*

evil treasure produces evil, for out of the abundance of the heart his mouth speaks.'" (Luke 6: 43-45)

Every tree bears the kind of fruit which that kind of tree bears, without exception. You will never see walnuts growing on a pear tree or pears growing on a grapevine. Pear trees grow pears. Walnut trees grow walnuts. Likewise, you will never see edible fruit growing on a plant that does not produce edible fruit, and vice versa. Because of that, fruit is a very good identifier of the plant itself. My husband is an avid gardener and can identify an extremely wide array of flora very easily. But at times, even he has to see what fruit particular plants have produced in order to correctly identify those particular plants. This is another purpose of fruit: identification.

FRUIT BEYOND THE PHYSICAL

Beyond the commonplace fruit trees, we are familiar with, including even some mentioned in the book of Genesis, such as the fig tree, it seems the intended purpose of the two focal-point trees in the garden that we have been discussing primarily in this book go beyond simple food production. The Tree of Life is not just merely a food source, but also produces life in those who eat it. Likewise, the Tree of the Knowledge of Good and Evil is not merely a food source, but also produces the fruit of knowledge of good and evil in those who eat it. While the fruit of any tree identifies the tree and carries the intent of reproduction, these two trees are special in that they also produce a non-tangible, identifiable, reproducible result in the person who consumes them.

Jesus also told a parable about seeds and the sower in Mark 4:1-20. Jesus tells the parable to the larger crowd, and later the disciples, Jesus' closest group of students, ask Him to explain its meaning. He explains that the seeds represent words of truth, and what happens when different people hear the truth based on the condition (or soil) of their hearts, their worldview, and access of the enemy in their lives. The same seed (truth) can produce abundantly, barely produce anything, or produce nothing at all, depending on the person, their choices, and surrounding circumstances and influences.

Adam and Eve ate the fruit of the Tree of the Knowledge of Good and Evil, not for the nourishment of their bodies, but for what they could gain from it; what it produced in them was knowledge of good and evil. That knowledge then produced death in them because of the condition of their hearts (self-centered desires combined with a lack of the fullness of understanding of the love of God), combined with the outside influence of the serpent's deception. This leads to their desire to disobey. It caused their immediate death as separation from the life source that is God, as well as their eventual physical death through separation from the Tree of Life. I believe God mandated this separation from the Tree of Life as a divine act of mercy so that they would not have to live in perpetual death and separation for all eternity.

> *"Then the Lord God said, 'Behold, the man has become like one of us in knowing good and evil. Now, lest he reach out his hand and take also of the tree of life and eat, and live forever—' therefore the Lord God sent him out from the garden of Eden to work the ground from which he was taken. He drove out the man, and at the east of the gar-*

den of Eden he placed the cherubim and a flaming sword
that turned every way to guard the way to the tree of life."
(Genesis 3:22-24)

Not everyone on this earth has access to ordinary fruit trees to eat
from for the nourishment of our bodies. However, we all have access to
eat of the Tree of the Knowledge of Good and Evil and the Tree of Life
(through the death and resurrection of Jesus Christ), and we all eat of
one or both daily, not by oral consumption, but through our thoughts,
actions, words, and choices. We reap the consequences of what we con-
sume, and the condition of our hearts dictates what reproduces in our
lives, and in everything and everyone around us.

CHAPTER 6
COVENANTS OF LAW AND GRACE

For thousands of years, humanity lived largely in separation from God, and without access to the Tree of Life. There were those who, despite everyone and everything around them, still pursued God (such as Enoch and Noah), and God rewarded them richly. There were also those whom God pursued (such as Abraham and Moses), through whom God began His plan to reveal Himself and to rescue humanity from bondage to sin, separation and death. God could have forced everyone to come to Him out of His love for them, knowing that it would be best for them, but even still He maintained the option of choice that only true love can give. But through Abraham, then through Moses and the Law, and eventually Jesus the Messiah, He began to woo humanity back to Himself, and provide a way back into relationship and right-standing with Himself.

RELATIONSHIP REESTABLISHED THROUGH COVENANT

God began this work of restoration through a common ancient practice of a legally binding relationship known as covenant, something that would have been familiar and understandable to the people with whom God was interacting. There are many different types of covenants, mostly beyond the scope of this book (and beyond my expertise), however, I want to focus on the three main types that carry the story of humanity through ancient and newer biblical texts and through today. The purpose of a covenant was to establish the type of relationship that would exist between two people or two groups of people. This would include any terms and conditions, or expectations, that would need to be met in order for that relationship to continue, and any qualifiers that would identify who was allowed to participate in the covenant. It sounds very complicated, however, think of a covenant in terms of a marriage relationship between a husband and wife or a treaty between two nations. Covenantal relationships can be incredibly intimate and personal, or merely a formal arrangement for the benefit of (usually) both parties.

GRANT COVENANT

So, God pursued Abraham and offered him the opportunity for relationship, a first major step in the process of restoring humanity to Himself. This was a legally binding relationship in the form of a covenant, practiced in a way that would have been familiar to Abraham.

The type of covenant God established with Abraham (and his descendants) is what we call a *grant covenant,* in which a greater, more powerful king blesses a lesser king. With a grant covenant, the burden of maintaining the covenant is put entirely on the greater king, meaning, there is nothing the lesser king could do to end the covenant. There were no major terms and conditions to uphold outside of a promise on the part of the greater king to bless the lesser (and his people).[1] If Abraham and his offspring wanted to be participants and beneficiaries in this covenant, the sign of their willingness was to circumcise every male in the household.[2] In other words, what qualified a person for participation in the Abrahamic Covenant was being an offspring of Abraham; what allowed them to receive the benefits of the covenant was circumcision. There was also no time limit or expiration, put on this covenant; it was to be an everlasting covenant, as the greater King, God, upon whom the covenant depends, lives forever.[3]

KINSHIP COVENANT

Fast forward several hundred years. The descendants of Abraham have become a great multitude and are enslaved by the people of Egypt. God raised up a leader for the Israelites in a man named Moses. He was raised in the house of Pharoah as a prince. Moses eventually learned of his true heritage, murdered an Egyptian in defense of an Israelite slave, ran away into the desert as a fugitive, and became the son-in-law of the priest of the Midianites. Forty years later, God called to him from a bush that was burning without being consumed and gave him the mandate to go back to Egypt and rescue the people of Israel from their slavery. Moses reluctantly agreed to go. Pharoah refused to let

---

1   Genesis 17:1-8

2   Genesis 17:9-14

3   "'And I will establish my covenant between me and you and your offspring after you throughout their generations for an everlasting covenant, to be God to you and to your offspring after you.'" (Genesis 17:7)

the Israelites leave, just as God said would happen, and Pharoah increased the workload of the Israelites. God then told Moses to offer the same grant covenant to the people of Israel that He had offered to Abraham,[4] but "they did not listen to Moses, because of their broken spirit and harsh slavery."[5] Nevertheless, God showed His power to the Egyptians through a series of ten plagues, after which the Israelites were finally allowed to leave. Pharoah regretted his decision immediately, pursued the people, and God opened a passageway through the Red Sea, allowing the people to cross freely on dry ground and burying the Egyptians underwater.

Although now truly free physically, the Israelites were still enslaved in their hearts and minds. God knew they did not have the capacity to accept unconditional blessing in the form of a grant covenant. Even though they were still beneficiaries of the Abrahamic Covenant, they were unable to accept a relationship with God without terms and conditions. So, God in His love for the people, lowered Himself and offered a lesser, but still amazing covenant called a *kinship covenant.* (Marriage is a type of kinship covenant.)

Kinship covenants were commonplace in that day, and were practiced extensively by the Egyptians, so this type of covenant would have been very familiar to the Israelites. Kinship covenants involved two equal kings (or in marriage, a man and a woman) who wished to establish a mutually beneficial relationship. Each party would bring a short list of expectations for the other party, that if not met, would signal the

---

4   Exodus 6:2-8

5   Exodus 6:9

end of the covenantal relationship. (In Israelite marriage, these expectations were called the *ketubah*, and were similar in some ways to Western marriage vows.) These expectations, or terms, were written in duplicate. Each of the two copies was then placed in a covenant box and placed in the temple of the god of each king. If one of the kings broke the covenant by breaking one of the terms of the covenant, it was the responsibility of that king's god to punish that king and his people.

So, the God of Israel lowered Himself to be an equal king in a kinship covenant with the people of Israel. He expressed His intent that all the people be a kingdom of priests in this covenant,[6] and asked them to prepare themselves as a bride would prepare herself for her husband.[7] The people initially agreed, but when they saw God in the lightning, thunder and smoke on the mountain, they refused to be equal participants in the covenant, and instead asked Moses to be the mediator between them and God.[8] Moses accepted and became the second king in the kinship covenant (God being the first king). God wrote ten commandments, or terms, in duplicate on two stone tablets. Much disobedience ensued. The people of Israel broke the covenant

---

6 "'You yourselves have seen what I did to the Egyptians, and how I bore you on eagles' wings and brought you to myself. Now therefore, if you will indeed obey my voice and keep my covenant, you shall be my treasured possession among all peoples, for all the earth is mine; and you shall be to me a kingdom of priests and a holy nation.'" (Exodus 19:4-6a)

7 Exodus 19:9-15

8 "Now when all the people saw the thunder and the flashes of lightning and the sound of the trumpet and the mountain smoking, the people were afraid and trembled, and they stood far off and said to Moses, 'You speak to us, and we will listen; but do not let God speak to us, lest we die.' 'Moses said to the people, 'Do not fear, for God has come to test you, that the fear of him may be before you, that you may not sin.' The people stood far off, while Moses drew near to the thick darkness where God was.'" (Exodus 20:18-21)

almost immediately, and Moses broke the stone tablets in anger.[9] But God in His mercy made a second set of stone tablets, giving the people another chance.

If both kings in the covenant were earthly, each king would have taken one of the tablets and placed it in a covenant box in their god's temple. But since God was both a king-participant and the God of the people, both tablets were placed in the same covenant box in the Tabernacle. God was now a participant in the covenant, as well as the God expected to enact punishment on the people if, and when, they broke the terms of the covenant. God, being righteous, *could not* break the covenant; doing so would be a violation of who He is: righteous. And now, because of the structure of this type of covenant, He was put in an awkward position where He had to punish the people when they disobeyed and broke the terms of this covenant; if He did not it would be in violation of who He is: righteous. Righteousness is being true and faithful to the covenant one is under. God can never act outside of the nature of who He is. God *is* not a punisher (as in, punishment is not at the core of *who He is*), but He *is* righteous, and as such, under the terms of the covenant, as God of the people, He had to punish transgressions to the covenant in order to be righteous.

Side note: This is why there appears to be such a dichotomy between how God appears to be in the Old Covenant (the covenant established through Moses) and the way Jesus spoke and acted. Jesus entered the Old Covenant as a man-participant, not as a god-participant, and was therefore able to express the heart and nature of God separate from

---

9   Exodus 32

God's role as punisher. In other words, Jesus was the example of how God would behave if He was only a *participant* in the Covenant, and not also the God and *enforcer* of the Covenant. Through His life and teachings, Jesus was also able to demonstrate and teach God's true intent in the Covenant and its laws, separate from people's wrong assumptions and additions to the Law.[10]

So, God set up a kinship covenant between Himself and Moses as a mediator of the people. God gave Moses exact plans for the building of a tabernacle (or tent) of worship, as well as instructions for every aspect of how a priest-led system of worship was expected to be run. God set up a system of sacrifices for the atonement (or covering) of individual sins, culminating in annual sacrifices for covering the sins of all of the people and the annual renewal of the covenant (called the Day of Atonement, or Yom Kippur). The people demonstrated early and often that their hearts were far from God, and that they would easily and repeatedly break the terms of this covenant. God wanted to remain in covenant with the people, so in His mercy, He created a way for this covenant to be renewed in spite of the disobedience of the people and their repeated breaking of this covenant through the annual sacrifice on the Day of Atonement. Unlike a grant covenant, the people were subject to the consequences of following or breaking this covenant, but by God's grace, the covenant itself could be renewed even after it had been broken.

---

10   In an attempt to clarify the Law of Moses, religious leaders added a lengthy set of rules that were required to be followed in addition to the original 613 laws laid out by Moses. These are known as the *Talmud* or *Oral Torah*. While the leaders may have had good intentions, they often missed God's heart and added unnecessary burden. In their desire to do everything "just right" before God, they became legalistic and missed the deeper truth of His heart of love.

VASSAL COVENANT

Moses traveled with the people through the wilderness for forty years, interceding on behalf of the people in the presence of God as they continually disobeyed Him. God knew that Moses' life on this earth would eventually come to an end, and with Moses' death (as a mediator and king number 2 in the covenant) would come to the end of the covenant itself. The people were still unwilling and unable to be direct participants in a covenant with God (they still could not accept a grant covenant) and continually showed themselves to be unable to remain faithful to the terms and conditions of a simple kinship covenant. God remembered His promises to bless the world through the descendants of Abraham (God was still faithful to His covenant with Abraham), and instead of allowing the kinship covenant to end at Moses' death, he downgraded the covenant to what is known as a *vassal covenant*. In a vassal covenant, a conquering king comes to the defeated people, now kingless, and says, "I could kill you all, but I won't. Here is a long list of rules and expectations. If you follow these, I will bless you and protect you; if you don't, these will be the consequences." God worked with Moses and expanded the original ten commandments to include a total of 613 laws, with explicit blessings for obedience and curses for disobedience. It sounds harsh, but the blessings always *far* outweighed the curses.[11] Also, the people knew what was expected of them, as opposed to neighboring kingdoms, who had little idea what their gods

---

11 "You shall not bow down to them or serve them, for I the Lord your God am a jealous God, visiting the iniquity of the fathers on the children to the third and the fourth generation of those who hate me, but showing steadfast love to thousands *[or, to the thousandth generation]* of those who love me and keep my commandments." (Exodus 20:5-6)

expected of them, except constant sacrifice, self-mutilation, etc., in hopes of *maybe* a blessing. (I think God also may have wanted to inspire obedience for the people's sake through their own built-in desire for blessing and fear of punishment.)

This downgraded vassal covenant is considered a continuation of the kinship covenant originally established through Moses, and both covenants are called collectively the Mosaic Covenant, or the Old Covenant. The terms and conditions of the Covenant are called the Law of Moses, and the books that describe the situation and stories surrounding the Old Covenant are called the *Torah*, which include the first five books of the Bible. A person's inclusion in the Old Covenant (what qualified him or her) was based on that person's (and the collective nation's) *performance* and obedience to the Law.

RELEASED FROM LAW AND FREE TO MARRY AGAIN

Fast forward through hundreds of years of mostly disobedience by the people of Israel. God sent prophet after prophet to warn the people of impending judgment. (The harshest consequences due to the people for disobedience to the Old Covenant were almost always delayed and often came following repeated warnings calling for repentance.) Through His prophets, God repeatedly compares the people to an unfaithful woman who constantly cheats on her husband (God). In Jeremiah chapter 3, God explains that because Israel has abandoned her covenant to Him and "married" another (through worship of other gods), He has issued Israel a certificate of divorce. In spite of God's hurt, anger, and disgust at Israel's unfaithfulness, He repeatedly expresses His desire for her return. No matter how unfaithful they have been, God still wants His people back, and never gives up pursuit of them. Under God's Law, the terms of the Old Covenant given through Moses, if a man divorces his wife and she marries another, and her second husband divorces her or dies, she cannot then return to her first husband; he is not allowed to take her back as his wife.[12] God, being righteous, cannot break His own covenant and re-marry Israel under the same covenant.

The first marriage covenant can only be broken through the death of the husband or wife:

> *"'For a married woman is bound by law to her husband while he lives, but if her husband dies she is released from the law of marriage. Accordingly, she will be called an adulteress if she lives with another man while her husband is alive. But if her husband dies, she is free from that law, and if she marries another man she is not an adulteress.'"*
> (Romans 7:2-3)

---

12   "When a man takes a wife and marries her, if then she finds no favor in his eyes because he has found some indecency in her, and he writes her a certificate of divorce and puts it in her hand and sends her out of his house, and she departs out of his house, and if she goes and becomes another man's wife, and the latter man hates her and writes her a certificate of divorce and puts it in her hand and sends her out of his house, or if the latter man dies, who took her to be his wife, then her former husband, who sent her away, may not take her again to be his wife, after she has been defiled, for that is an abomination before the Lord . And you shall not bring sin upon the land that the Lord your God is giving you for an inheritance." (Deuteronomy 24:1-4)

In order for God to marry Israel again and enter into a new marriage with her, He would have to die to end the first covenant and be raised to life again in order for a new covenant to be established.

Through the prophet, Jeremiah, God lays out his intent to form a new covenant:

> *"Behold, the days are coming, declares the Lord , when I will make a new covenant with the house of Israel and the house of Judah, not like the covenant that I made with their fathers on the day when I took them by the hand to bring them out of the land of Egypt, my covenant that they broke, though I was their husband, declares the Lord. For this is the covenant that I will make with the house of Israel after those days, declares the Lord: I will put my law within them, and I will write it on their hearts. And I will be their God, and they shall be my people. And no longer shall each one teach his neighbor and each his brother, saying, 'Know the Lord,' for they shall all know me, from the least of them to the greatest, declares the Lord. For I will forgive their iniquity, and I will remember their sin no more.'"*
> (Jeremiah 31:31-34)

And:

> *"And they shall be my people, and I will be their God. I will give them one heart and one way, that they may fear me forever, for their own good and the good of their children after them. I will make with them an everlasting covenant, that I will not turn away from doing good to them. And I will*

put the fear of me in their hearts, that they may not turn from me. I will rejoice in doing them good, and I will plant them in this land in faithfulness, with all my heart and all my soul.'" (Jeremiah 32:38-41)

God's intent for this new covenant was that it would be an everlasting covenant, one unlike the first (referring to the Old, Mosaic Covenant). This would be an unbreakable covenant, established through Jesus Christ, the Messiah, the promised one. Being both fully God and fully man,[13] Jesus' death would end the first covenant, dying in God's place (since God Himself cannot die) as well as dying in the place of humanity, freeing both God and the people from its legal bond. Being without sin, His death would be an atonement sacrifice for the sins of the people, not just *covering* the sins (as the sacrifice of animals would do under the Old Covenant) but *removing* them entirely, allowing the children of Adam and Eve to return fully into right-standing in the presence of God. And by His death, resurrection, and blood, Jesus would also simultaneously establish a brand-new covenant between Himself (as the representative and mediator for the people) and God, the Father.

This New Covenant is a covenant unlike any other. It is a kinship covenant in that it is between God the Father and God the Son, unbreakable because of the very nature and righteousness of God Himself (since He, being righteous, cannot break a covenant). It is also most

---

13   "Have this mind among yourselves, which is yours in Christ Jesus, who, though he was in the form of God, did not count equality with God a thing to be grasped, but emptied himself, by taking the form of a servant, being born in the likeness of men. And being found in human form, he humbled himself by becoming obedient to the point of death, even death on a cross." (Philippians 2:5-8)

like a grant covenant between God as the greater King, blessing Jesus as the lesser King, who being fully human, also made a way for us to be included in (or beneficiaries of) this new covenantal relationship. Like the Abrahamic covenant, participation in this covenant and its blessings also comes with the sign of circumcision, except in this case it is a circumcision not of the flesh, but of the heart.[14] How does one circumcise the heart? By belief.[15] By belief alone can anyone participate in the New Covenant, and we receive the benefits by the grace of the greatest King. Our lives then manifest our new position in God as we learn and grow to be more like Him and His self-sacrificial love and the life that it brings.

---

14   Romans 4

15   "Then he brought them out and said, "Sirs, what must I do to be saved?" And they said, "Believe in the Lord Jesus, and you will be saved, you and your household." (Acts 16:30-31)

CHAPTER 7
WHAT DOES THIS HAVE TO DO WITH ME?

In the last chapter, we discussed three of the main covenants in the Bible: The Abrahamic Covenant, the Mosaic or Old Covenant, and the New Covenant. Each covenant establishes a defined relationship and its benefits to one or both parties, each with its own qualifiers for what allows a person (or nation) to be a legal participant in that covenant. Perhaps you are starting to connect the dots and see your place within all this, or perhaps, if you're like me, you can use a little help. Covenants, like sacrifices, are not something we tend to think about often (or at all) these days, unless you have been a part of the occult or live in a nation where these practices are still common. As believers in a Western nation, we tend to be fairly removed from the concepts, and therefore tend to gloss over the meanings and implications for the people we read about in Scripture, and for our own lives. Or, we could lump all the covenants and their implications into the same box and come up with some wacky theologies that actually pull us away from God, rather than draw us toward Him. Regardless of what theological box you find yourself in, climb out for a moment and consider the implications of all we are discussing on your own position with God and the full gambit of your beliefs about God, life, the Bible, etc.

One thing that helped me wrap my head around the implications of the major covenants in the Bible is a short book by Chad M. Mansbridge, called *He Qualifies You!* In the book he explains the three main covenants we have discussed simply, and in more detail. I would highly recommend reading it! He makes the case that:

- Under the Abrahamic Covenant, the qualifier for inclusion and blessing is a person's *Pedigree*.

- Under the Old Covenant, the qualifier for inclusion and blessing was a person's *Performance*.

- Under the New Covenant, the qualifier for inclusion and blessing is a person's *Position*.

I realize the verb tense is inconsistent in those statements, however that is intentional.

POSITION VS. PERFORMANCE

We have been given the gift of inclusion in the New Covenant, and therefore, are beneficiaries of all God's promised blessings as our right and our inheritance. It is not due to us having earned that right, but it is due to our *position in Jesus* (through belief in Him), because of all *He* did on our behalf, and the fact that He has included us in His inheritance (we are His inheritance, He is our inheritance, and we are co-heirs of all things with Him).[1] His righteousness and right-standing before God becomes our righteousness and right-standing before God when we are positioned in Him. It is His free gift to us. It cannot be earned, only received. Our sin (and separation from God) positions us to earn the wage of death, but Jesus' self-sacrificial love paid the wage of death we deserve, canceling the record of death[2] and allowing for our inclusion with Him in God.[3] His gift is not a covering of our sin (as the blood of animals covered sin in the Old Covenant), but He died *as us,* and was raised to eternal life *as us,* and when we are baptized, we are displaying our inclusion with Him in His death and resurrection.[4] That old sin nature is now dead and buried; now we can live fully immersed in the life of Jesus.[5]

Many believers tend to become confused trying to include themselves in the Old Covenant and its system of law as a means to *earn* a position with God through *performance.* The laws dictated in the Law of Moses, especially the first ten commandments, are especially good

---

1   "The Spirit himself bears witness with our spirit that we are children of God, and if children, then heirs—heirs of God and fellow heirs with Christ, provided we suffer with him in order that we may also be glorified with him." (Romans 8:16-17)

2   "And you, who were dead in your trespasses and the uncircumcision of your flesh, God made alive together with him, having forgiven us all our trespasses, by canceling the record of debt that stood against us with its legal demands. This he set aside, nailing it to the cross." (Colossians 2:13-14)

3   "For the wages of sin is death, but the free gift of God is eternal life in Christ Jesus our Lord." (Romans 6:23)

4   "...having been buried with him in baptism, in which you were also raised with him through faith in the powerful working of God, who raised him from the dead." (Colossians 2:12)

5   "I have been crucified with Christ. It is no longer I who live, but Christ who lives in me. And the life I now live in the flesh I live by faith in the Son of God, who loved me and gave himself for me." (Galatians 2:20)

in that they show us what God deems right and wrong, resulting in a life that resembles the blessings of inclusion in God. However, it is helpful to understand that these laws were established with a specific people group, in a specific historical context, that we may or may not understand at face value without that historical understanding. It is also imperative to understand that these laws were given as a part of the terms and conditions of a person's inclusion in a very specific covenantal relationship, a covenantal relationship that is now null and void:

> *"Or do you not know, brothers—for I am speaking to those who know the law—that the law is binding on a person only as long as he lives? For a married woman is bound by law to her husband while he lives, but if her husband dies she is released from the law of marriage. Accordingly, she will be called an adulteress if she lives with another man while her husband is alive. But if her husband dies, she is free from that law, and if she marries another man she is not an adulteress. Likewise, my brothers, you also have died to the law through the body of Christ, so that you may belong to another, to him who has been raised from the dead, in order that we may bear fruit for God. For while we were living in the flesh, our sinful passions, aroused by the law, were at work in our members to bear fruit for death. But now we are released from the law, having died to that which held us captive, so that we serve in the new way of the Spirit and not in the old way of the written code."* (Romans 7:1-6)

What Paul is saying here is that when Jesus died, He died to the Law, ending participation in the Old Covenant; we died with Him, so to return to the Old Covenant through performance to the Law would be akin to adultery!

Does that mean that the Law of Moses is bad? Absolutely not! It was a *huge* step forward for humanity in returning to relationship with God and a *huge* step away from the effects of our own self-understanding of good and evil. We can still learn immensely from its tenants and principles. And there are times in our lives where it would be absolutely advantageous for us to apply its laws to areas in our lives where it is needed, but only in the way that wisdom dictates, and not as a means to *perform* and *earn* our way into right-standing with God. To try and earn our way to God through performance is to say all that Jesus did for us was not enough, that more needed to be done, and that somehow, we are capable of adding to the works of Christ! Think about the audacity of that! Rather, our thoughts and behavior should be a reflection of our position in God, and a means of worship out of gratitude for our salvation from sin, death and separation from God, and a true reflection of all He is.

OLD COVENANT LAW VS. OTHER LAWS

Everyone on Earth, regardless of religious or personal belief, abides by some kind of law. In other words, we all do what we deem to be right in our own minds, individually and collectively. Often times, our laws are harmful to ourselves or others, but mostly, our laws are beneficial and help maintain order between people and in our own lives. Many of our laws are based on Biblical principles, like: do not murder, or do not steal. We also have governmental laws against driving too fast, zoning laws, tax laws, and on and on. We have laws for ourselves based on our own beliefs about morality. (e.g. Is lying right or wrong? Is stealing right or wrong and under what circumstances?) We also have personally applied laws that we must implement in order to be functional and survive in society, such as going to bed by a certain time so that we don't sleep through the next day and get fired from our jobs. These kinds of laws, while coupled with Godly wisdom, are generally good and beneficial to us and others around us. Law in itself is not necessarily bad, and often it is imperatively necessary in a fallen world.

Applying law to our personal lives is wise, in fact, especially when we are young and immature in faith, as it helps us to grow and mature. But we must never live under law as a means of earning anything from God, making ourselves right before God, etc. No amount of law or performance can ever change your position in God. No amount of law or performance can ever alter His nature and posture of love for you. The only thing that changes your position in or out of Him is your choice to believe.

TO KEEP THE LAW OF MOSES IS TO RETURN TO THE OLD COVENANT

We do not ever want to enter into the Old Covenant once again, because to do so would be to violate the New Covenant. Paul said to the Galatians, "For if you are trying to make yourselves right with God by keeping the law, you have been cut off from Christ! You have fallen away from God's grace." (Galatians 5:4 NLT) Not only does following the Law to make ourselves right before God avail us nothing, Paul says,

> *"Rather, I am a sinner if I rebuild the old system of law I already tore down. For when I tried to keep the law, it condemned me. So I died to the law—I stopped trying to meet all its requirements—so that I might live for God."*
> (Galatians 2:18-19 NLT)

Paul, who had followed the Law to the letter from birth, stopped trying to meet all its requirements! Under the terms and conditions of the Law, that would put him in violation to the covenant and in violation to God, but Paul knew that God was no longer honoring the Old Covenant, and by continuing to operate under the Law, he would be condemning himself and excluding himself from the far superior New Covenant.[6]

The Old only gave a way for the covering of sins; the New provides complete elimination of sins along with the cleansing of our consciences.[7] The Old was conditional and had to be renewed continually with the blood of animal sacrifices; the New is unconditional and has been established eternally through a one-time sacrifice, making the need for further sacrifices unnecessary, and making the Old Covenant obso-

---

6 "But as it is, Christ has obtained a ministry that is as much more excellent than the old as the covenant he mediates is better, since it is enacted on better promises." (Hebrews 8:6)

7 "...how much more will the blood of Christ, who through the eternal Spirit offered himself without blemish to God, purify our conscience from dead works to serve the living God." (Hebrews 9:14)

lete.[8] Why would we despise what Jesus did for us and cut ourselves off from Him, only to go back to a Covenant that is inferior and obsolete?

To return to the Old Covenant is to return to the curses of the Law.[9] One must follow *all* of the laws in their entirety, or he is in violation of all of the Law, or therefore, subject to its curses.[10] The curses that come as a result of breaking the Law are not minor! They include sickness, death, destruction, and victory over us by our enemies. And it is impossible now for you to fulfill every one of the 613 commandments, so no matter what you do you will be in violation of the Law and subject to its curses. You would have to make every sacrifice in the temple (which was destroyed in 70 A.D.) through a Levitical priest (Levites can no longer prove their lineage as required under the Law because the genealogical records were destroyed along with the temple in 70 A.D.). The temple system was destroyed, so *no one on earth* has been able to fulfill every requirement of the Law since 70 A.D.! Furthermore, to return to animal sacrifices would mean a complete rejection of Jesus, who is the one sacrifice to end all sacrifices. There are some who try and follow as much of the Law as they are able, but no one can follow every single commandment. This means no matter what you do, if you place yourself under the Law by trying to follow even some of the Law, you are in violation of *all* of the Law, and therefore, subject to its curses.

---

8 "In speaking of a new covenant, he makes the first one obsolete. And what is becoming obsolete and growing old is ready to vanish away." (Hebrews 8:13)

9 "For all who rely on works of the law are under a curse; for it is written, 'Cursed be everyone who does not abide by all things written in the Book of the Law, and do them.'" (Galatians 3:10)

10 "For whoever keeps the whole law but fails in one point has become guilty of all of it." (James 2:10)

As you can see, the implications of our beliefs and our attempts to justify ourselves according to the Law are massive! Perhaps, in our good intention to honor God and make ourselves right before Him, we are either knowingly or unknowingly submitting ourselves to the Law. Perhaps that is why we are still seeing the consequences of sin and death, consequences that Jesus paid for, consequences we do not have to suffer. Perhaps that is why we have not yet seen the full manifestation of the blessings promised to us as a part of the New Covenant. Yet, we in our pride, thinking we know what is right and good to do before God, still believe we have to clean ourselves up, and start following the Law before we can come to Him and accept His free gift of Jesus' righteousness, given in grace. What arrogance!

WRESTLING WITH TWO TREES AND TWO COVENANTS

However, we are not alone in this struggle between the two covenants. It is essentially the same decision that Adam and Eve faced in the Garden of Eden. The Law of Sin and Death, the Old Covenant, is rooted in the Tree of the Knowledge of Good and Evil. It had to be, or the people could not accept it because of the harshness of their slavery to sin and death. They did not have the capacity to receive a gift given in grace, undeserved. Yet God met them where they were and offered a signpost showing the way out, the way to Himself. To Abraham, God gave the blessings of a promise to be given to his offspring, and to the Israelites, walking through the mirey depths of slavery, He gave the

Law as a tutor and guide.[11] Much of the New Testament deals with the working out of these covenants, the differences, meanings and implications.[12] We are not alone in wrestling with these ideas!

When Adam and Eve ate from the Tree of Knowledge, God had to block them from eating of the Tree of Life, lest they live forever in a state of death and separation. When we participate in the Old Covenant by trying to earn our way to God through our performance, we choose to eat from the Tree of Knowledge and the system that was established through its initial consumption. Even though our actions might reflect what God says is right and good, we are still operating under that Tree. It is a tree that is earned through doing, through taking, through attaining what is in it for me, through *performance*.

When we try to earn our way to God, it is always for personal gain. When we instead lay down our desires, even desires for Him and for good things, and submit to God and His desires and ways, then we are posturing ourselves to be able to receive. We cannot receive something freely that we have earned. But we must trust that God is good and that He is righteous and will fulfill everything that He has promised.

---

11   "Now the promises were made to Abraham and to his offspring. It does not say, "And to offsprings," referring to many, but referring to one, "And to your offspring," who is Christ. This is what I mean: the law, which came 430 years afterward, does not annul a covenant previously ratified by God, so as to make the promise void. For if the inheritance comes by the law, it no longer comes by promise; but God gave it to Abraham by a promise. Why then the law? It was added because of transgressions, until the offspring should come to whom the promise had been made, and it was put in place through angels by an intermediary." (Galatians 3:16-19)

12   The early church leaders were asking questions such as: What are the implications if we follow only part of the Law? What do we require of those who never knew the Law and never participated in the Old Covenant, yet believe in Jesus? What do we keep from the Old? Do we keep any of it?

Jesus summarized the Ten Commandments, the foundation of the Old Covenant in this way:

"You shall love the Lord your God with all your heart and with all your soul and with all your mind. This is the great and first commandment. And a second is like it: You shall love your neighbor as yourself. On these two commandments depend all the Law and the Prophets." (Matthew 22:37b-40)

In other words, love with everything you have within you. Love with everything you know to do. If everyone did this, the world would be a *far* better place! It is very good, but it is action-based, performance-based. It is also dependent on you, and what you have in you, your capabilities, your limitations, your faults, your lack, even your perception of what love is. But it was a very, very good place to start!

Contrary to that, yet complimentary and far greater, Jesus later gave only one commandment to show us what the fruit of our lives should look like when we are positioned in Him in the New Covenant: "This is my commandment, that you love one another as I have loved you. Greater love has no one than this, that someone lay down his life for his friends. You are my friends if you do what I command you." (John 15:12-14) In other words, love as Jesus loved. Easier said than done, you say? Of course! Loving as Jesus loved cannot be dependent on you at all but has to be dependent on Him alone. It can *only* be received! It is *His* love working *through* you as a conduit, as a leaking, overflowing vessel, in response to Him and with Him. It is all about, and only about, your *position* in Him.

That, my friends, is the Tree of Life. It can only be received as a free gift, it can never be earned, it can never be stolen, only abandoned, and it can only be accessed through Jesus Christ.

Like every aspect of the Old Covenant, the veil leading to the Holy of Holies in the Tabernacle, and later the Temple, was designed to be earthly reflections of a heavenly reality that point to Jesus and the New Covenant. On these curtains were sewn two cherubim, to reflect the cherubim with the flaming sword who blocked access to the Tree of Life in the Garden of Eden. The flaming sword would kill any who passed through. Jesus compared His body to that veil; when it was torn, when He was killed, the way was made for free access into the Holy of Holies, God's dwelling place, the place of His presence, and access to the Tree of Life. When Jesus died, He died *as* us, not only *for* us. When He died, we died with Him, if we are willing to participate with Him in His death by laying down our lives (our wants, our desires, our self-centered motives and intents), dying to everything we were never created to be in the first place.[13] When we do that, then we can also participate with Him in His resurrection into a brand new life,[14] where we find that which we have always longed for all our lives but never realized: Him. And He becomes our inheritance, our life, blessings overflowing and full of glory beyond comparison!

---

13   "Whoever finds his life will lose it, and whoever loses his life for my sake will find it." (Matthew 10:39)

14   "We were buried therefore with him by baptism into death, in order that, just as Christ was raised from the dead by the glory of the Father, we too might walk in newness of life." (Romans 6:4)

CHAPTER 8
LAW AS A TUTOR

"Now wait a minute!" I hear some of you screaming in your heads, "But we need the Law! We can't just have lawlessness!" Just as every child born with a sin-nature needs to learn obedience through submission to rules laid out by the parents, we all at times need to be reminded what God says is right and wrong and submit ourselves to His authority, trusting that what He says is good and right will be the best thing for us, even though the world around us is shouting otherwise. We might experience freedom through the grace of God (like a drug addict who finds healing from his addiction and no longer desires the drugs that held him captive for so many years), but in another area of our lives, we may need the wisdom to know when to abstain from something that may not be harmful to another person (like a person addicted to pornography who needs accountability software on his or her computer, or cannot even keep a computer in the house at all). Just as the Law of Moses was a good tutor for the people of Israel (and the world around them), teaching us what a Godly life looks like when lived out, there is often a benefit in applying wisdom to our lives and knowing when and where to apply law.

One person may experience the freedom to drink a glass of wine every day with dinner; another may need to limit consumption to one glass a week; another may not be able to drink anything alcoholic at all; another may need to avoid being around anyone else having a drink in order to avoid falling back into alcoholism. Godly love would dictate that the first person would gladly give up his nightly glass of wine on behalf of the conscience of the last, knowing how harmful that same glass of wine would be in his life.

There is a *tremendous* difference between *applying law in wisdom* to areas of our life that need growth in order to properly reflect the God we serve (and to learn the way He loves) and *following the Law out of performance* for the purposes of making ourselves right before God. For some, wisdom would say to avoid eating pork because it is bad for your health. Others might avoid eating pork because it was forbidden in the Law, and they are fearful that eating pork would anger God or somehow jeopardize their position with Him. But a person who refuses to eat pork as a guest at someone's house for either reason may also be missing a much greater reality: the love, honor and grace for the host who may not have the same convictions.

The difference is in *why* and *how* you are applying law. We all apply law to our lives. Some apply Godly wisdom with the laws we choose to follow. Some apply law out of fear and misplaced belief. Some apply law unconsciously. But we all apply law. What are we hoping to attain by applying law? Are we trying to make ourselves right before God out of our own strength and power? Or are we applying wisdom to our lives, and presenting ourselves before God in rest, trusting that He is the only one who can bring about true healing and restoration? (Remember Eve's sin was in trying to attain something for herself rather than receiving from God.)

Receiving from God takes patience and trust. Often, He cannot give us what we want or need when we are actively trying to earn that thing because we know (consciously or unconsciously) that we have earned it somehow, which produces pride in our hearts, and pulls us away from Him. Receiving a gift does not require action, it requires posture. Action is performance and results in earned wages; posture is position, and results in openness to receive from the gift-giver when we are positioned in Him. We may apply law to an area of our lives in wisdom, knowing that that law positions us facing toward God and away from sin. We also must understand that no gift can ever be demanded, and sometimes, that thing we want may not be the best thing for us; sometimes, a greater good is produced in us through lack and suffering than through abundance. (Let that sink in for a moment!) Other times, it is through abundance, knowing we are undeserving, that God produces the greatest good in us.

God cares first and foremost about our relationship with Him; hand-in-hand with that is our position in Him, allowing Him the freedom to bless us, love on us, and grow in us. He is concerned with our material comforts to the degree that He loves us and knows all our needs; however, He will never grant us material comforts at the expense of the condition of our hearts, which directly affects our relationship and position with Him. His love holds nothing back for Himself, but gives everything on behalf of others, and sometimes God will expect and ask the same thing from us as His children. Often, we may not understand that that is what God is doing through us when we experience lack and suffering: loving others around us. (And sometimes we experience lack and suffering due to the self-serving actions of those around us living apart from God or making choices according to their own self-made version of "right" and "wrong.") The bottom line is that we must trust Him whether or not He chooses to provide the change we need or the things we want in the way we hope and expect. We must submit to His will, knowing He knows far more than we do, and trust that He is good. No matter what. Our job is merely to just *be* in Him, and from that place we live.

Sometimes, we must apply law to our lives because we are divided in our desire to serve God or serve ourselves. We must discipline ourselves as we live in an undisciplined world and hear constant voices contrary to the wisdom of God. We often get caught up when we shift subtly from resting in our position in Him, to performing, not just for Him but for the people around us. Much of what drives us as humans is our fear of what other people think and fear of how they might see us. But we cannot really listen to two people talking at once. Fear of man (fear of any kind, really) is never conquered by fighting the fear, by trying not to listen to its voice. Rather, we must fully turn our attention to God, turning our back on all the distractions, allowing the sheer magnitude of His awesomeness to completely overwhelm any other lesser fear or desire.

Often, this is a process, sometimes lengthy, as we gradually allow the sin-nature within us that wants to seek its selfish desires, to wither and die. Often this is a process of disciplined application of God's Word, His Truth, applied thoroughly to our minds and hearts until our belief system is truly pruned and honed to match His heart.[1] But it is a

---

1   "Do not be conformed to this world, but be transformed by the renewal of your mind..." (Romans 12:2a)

process of surrender to Him, not a process of earning or attaining.[2] He is the Master Gardener, pruning the dead branches off the vines of our hearts;[3] the vine itself cannot remove its own branches, and left to its own devices, will grow wild and unfruitful.

So no, law is not bad in itself, but it must be applied through a posture of surrender to Him, and not as a means of earning relationship or position with Him. We must not go back to slavery to a system of dos and don'ts[4] in mere hope of God's favor on us. We must receive freely His gift of right-standing and position in Him, and learn to rest freely in Him, surrendered to His pruning and guidance, becoming ever conformed to His image and likeness.[5]

---

2   Romans 8

3   John 15:1-11

4   "For freedom Christ has set us free; stand firm therefore, and do not submit again to a yoke of slavery." (Galatians 5:1, referring to the Law of Moses)

5   "For those whom he foreknew he also predestined to be conformed to the image of his Son, in order that he might be the firstborn among many brothers. And those whom he predestined he also called, and those whom he called he also justified, and those whom he justified he also glorified." (Romans 8:29-30)

CHAPTER 9
LOVE IS THE GREATER WAY

Jesus was asked by the religious leaders of His day, "Which is the greatest commandment in the Law?" He replied brilliantly by summarizing the entirety of the Law and everything spoken by God's prophets by summarizing the Ten Commandments, saying, "You shall love the Lord your God with all your heart and with all your soul and with all your mind. This is the great and first commandment. And a second is like it: You shall love your neighbor as yourself. On these two commandments depend all the Law and the Prophets."[1] Or in other words, love God with everything in you, and love your neighbor the way you love yourself and you will fulfill every requirement of the Law. Love is the very foundation of the Law of Moses and the Old Covenant.

The difficulty lies in the kind of love that is in us in our fallen state, separate from the source of true love, God Himself. Can someone love God when the only love they know is a self-serving, self-centered kind of "love?" Can we love others when we don't even have the capacity to love ourselves? Maybe we can in part; we can definitely love to the best of our own ability if we try really hard and learn as much as we can from God's law and teachers. But what does love look like when lived

---

1 Matthew 22:34-40

out? In our selfishness, we all have radically different ideas of what love looks like in action, which is where the specifics of the Law were helpful. Loving God looks like not honoring any other gods aside from the One True God, not making idols, keeping the name of God holy, and honoring a Sabbath day of rest. Loving others looks like not stealing, not lying, honoring your parents, not cheating on your spouse, etc.

"But what does rest from work on the Sabbath actually mean?" people have asked. "How does one go about doing that well? What qualifies as work? Lighting a fire must qualify as work, so we can't do that. Technically, when you flip a switch to turn on a lightbulb, it's kind of like starting a fire since electricity is involved, so maybe that would qualify as 'work' as well, so just in case, we better not do that on the Sabbath. We've got to do things absolutely, 100% right before the Lord, no mistakes! No room for error!"

Do you hear the striving to work to achieve in all that? Resting from work on the Sabbath in that way sounds like a lot of work to me! (And where is the love in that??) That is what happened as people became more and more driven to define the Law, to do things just right, adding more and more laws to clarify what the original Law meant. These were man-made additions to the Law, known as the *Oral Torah* or *Talmud*. What began as a law of love gradually became more and more complicated and works-driven over the centuries.

When Jesus came on the scene, He was born as one under the Law and honored and upheld every aspect of the Law as given by God to Moses. (The Law, the contractual agreement of the Old Covenant, did not end until Jesus' death and the subsequent destruction of the temple and temple system in 70 A.D.) But He did not honor or follow the man-made additions to the Law. That is part of what infuriated the religious leaders of the time. For example, one of the man-made laws stated that you could not harvest grain on the Sabbath, since that was considered work, so when Jesus' disciples (or students) picked heads of wheat to eat as they walked, the religious leaders were indignant and accused Jesus of not following or enforcing the Law with His disciples.[2] Jesus explained to the religious leaders that they were essentially missing the point of the Sabbath; they wanted to do the right thing, but were missing God's heart in the Law. Jesus came to fulfill the Law, and in doing so, He also revealed God's heart and intent in the Law: love.

The Law (as it was originally given) was intended to show the people (in their separation from God) what God's love looks like in action: love God and others with everything in you, and treat others as well as you treat yourself. Those ideas are still works-based, but it is what a people operating under a slave based mindset could handle. Work is very familiar to a slave, and earning blessings from God through work makes sense. People with a slave-mindset, under the system of the Tree of Knowledge (even those who are trying to do the right thing), will always tend to make things more complicated and difficult than they even need to, by trying and working harder. Or they just give up and say it's all too hard to do. In a way, that second group is right: it is too hard, or at least it feels like it sometimes for all of us. We all know what we are capable of doing on our best day, and we all know when we fail to live up to our best. We all have days where we fail. A system of performance is dependent on us living up to our absolute best at every

---

2   Mark 2:23-28

moment of every day in some kind of self-made, occasionally attainable perfection. And when we are on our best behavior, works give rise to the pride of accomplishment. So, either way, we fail.

In our consciences, we condemn ourselves every time we do fail, and sometimes we fail often. We frequently assume that our self-condemnation is from God[3] when really it is just another man-made construct of our own creation. Self-condemnation is ultimately just another form of pride, as it puts the focus back on our works and failures and prohibits us from receiving the full grace of His salvation, and His declaration of the Truth of who we are. Jesus came to save the world and to speak the Truth. When we reject the Truth as spoken by Jesus, we reject the Speaker of those words, and it is our own action of rejection that condemns us. We are judged, not by Jesus, not by God, but by the Truth itself. Jesus said, "If anyone hears my words and does not keep them, I do not judge him; for I did not come to judge the world but to save the world. The one who rejects me and does not receive my words has a judge; the word that I have spoken will judge him on the last day." (John 12:47-48) We are judged by the Truth as spoken by Jesus. While we may live in our own condemnation here on this Earth, by God's grace, we are not set up to be our own ultimate judge. Truth becomes our judge. Thankfully, otherwise, I believe we would all judge ourselves far more harshly than any judgment we could receive from God. But when Truth is our judge, what matters is less about what we do or don't do, and more about Who we accept or reject and what we believe; our actions merely indicate what we truly believe.

---

3   "For God did not send his Son into the world to condemn the world, but in order that the world might be saved through him." (John 3:17)

A HIGHER WAY

Jesus accomplished far more in His short life on Earth than we could possibly discuss. The apostle John said, "Now there are also many other things that Jesus did. Were every one of them to be written, I suppose that the world itself could not contain the books that would be written." (John 21:25) One of the major things He did was to fulfill the Law as God gave it while revealing God's heart, His love, in the Law. We would do well to follow the Law with God's love. But there is an even higher way!

Arguably, the greatest task Jesus accomplished was to establish the New Covenant through His death and resurrection, allowing humanity a return to right-standing relationship and position in God. There are two words in the original New Testament Greek for the word "new." The first is *neos* (νέος), meaning: *something young and youthful, or new and fresh*. The second, which is used in the phrase "New Covenant," is the word *kainos* (καινός), which means: *new in quality or innovation, as in, never found like this before*. Neos refers to a refreshing of the old, like a new moon or new wine; or, "my wagon broke down, so I need to get a new one." Kainos, on the other hand, would be not just a new wagon that looks like the old, but rather an interstellar, time traveling vehicle with invisibility technology: something that has never before been seen or found in existence anywhere. In other words, the New Covenant is not merely a replacement for the Old, but rather an entirely new, never-before-seen creation all its own. If the Old Covenant is the flame on a candle whose light can be seen from every seat of a stadium in the dark, then the New Covenant would be the electric lights of the stadium at full brightness. While the Old was spectacular, what Jesus established in the New Covenant far surpasses the Old:

> *"Now if the ministry of death, carved in letters on stone, came with such glory that the Israelites could not gaze at Moses' face because of its glory, which was being brought to an end, will not the ministry of the Spirit have even more glory? For if there was glory in the ministry of condemnation, the ministry of righteousness must far exceed it in glory. Indeed, in this case, what once had glory has come to have no glory at all, because of the glory that surpasses it. For if what was being brought to an end came with glory, much more will what is permanent have glory."*
> (2 Corinthians 3:7-11)

And with this New Covenant, Jesus establishes a new law of love: "A new commandment I give to you, that you love one another: just as I have loved you, you also are to love one another." (John 13:34) The word "new" in the Greek text here is the word kainos, meaning this is a commandment unlike anything commanded before. While the Old was marked by a love mustered up from within oneself through actions to earn one's own right-standing with God, this new commandment is marked by the laying down of oneself for the benefit of another, not through self-striving love but by allowing His love to work through us (as co-participants) as we abide in the gift of right-standing relationship in Him. In other words, this kind of love is a *response* to position instead of a means to *earn* position.

Jesus gives the new command to love as He has loved, and goes on to say, "By this all people will know that you are my disciples, if you have love for one another." (John 13:35) The Old Covenant commands were the terms of the Covenant, and if those terms were broken (or not obeyed), that would signal the end of the Covenant, if not renewed annually on the Day of Atonement.[4] The New Covenant is an eternal covenant,[5] meaning it cannot be broken, meaning there are no terms or conditions needing to be met in order to maintain that covenant, and there is no need for annual sacrifice because Jesus paid the price once and for all. Jesus gives the command to love as He loved, not as a condition for inclusion in the covenant, but as a signpost for others to mark your position in God's love; indeed, it is a natural consequence of that position in Jesus as we begin to reflect God's nature more and more.

Furthermore, if we are to receive the free gift of the self-less love of God through Jesus, allowing it to change us in our self-centered ways, and expressing Him in our love in all aspects of our life, we will fulfill the heart behind every one of the Laws of Moses. Would God's love murder? Never, rather it would strive to bring life! Would it steal? No, it would give in abundance! Is His love ever jealous of what another has? No way! It would celebrate the victories, accomplishments, and earnings of another as if they were its own.

So, what does this new kind of love look like? It looks and acts and sounds like Jesus. That is why the phrase, What Would Jesus Do

---

4   As a Kinship/Vassal Covenant

5   As a Grant Covenant between God and Jesus

(W.W.J.D.), was so popular not long ago; it was a reminder to live every moment as Jesus would, reacting in all situations with the love of Christ. It is a selfless kind of love that prioritizes others above ourselves. There are many examples of what this love looks like in action in the letters from the apostles to the newly formed churches in the first century after Jesus' resurrection. The most famous of all is 1 Corinthians 13, especially verses 4-7: "Love is patient and kind; love does not envy or boast; it is not arrogant or rude. It does not insist on its own way; it is not irritable or resentful; it does not rejoice at wrongdoing, but rejoices with the truth. Love bears all things, believes all things, hopes all things, endures all things." Romans 12 is another very practical list of examples. The important thing is to love like God loves as demonstrated by Jesus. It sometimes takes a while to learn that kind of love and unlearn our selfish ways of loving, so be patient with yourself; God is exceedingly patient with you. God cannot love you less than He is, and He is love. His love will always pursue you, wooing you to Himself and out of the void of Himself (and all things evil). The best way to learn His love is by spending time with Him, reading about Him with Him, talking to Him, listening to Him, engaging Him always and in every situation. Be a child and ask Him loads of questions (He loves that!). Just don't give up, always pursue His love, and allow Him and His transformational love to overtake you.

GRACE, SIN AND BELIEF

Whenever my husband or I teach on the subject of the free gift of love and the grace of God toward us as something to be received and not something to be earned through works, we inevitably find some who claim we are teaching "hyper-grace." (Can anyone have too much grace? Not me! But I digress...) The heart behind the accusation is usually one of desire to honor God through obedience to His Law, and a fear that grace will be used as a license to continue living apart from God, which I understand, but it is still a works and achievement-driven mindset. It is ultimately fueled by fear. I do get it. It's a terrible thing to see a loved one living a death-like life devoid of God (and all things good), especially if the person uses God's grace as an excuse to continue on as the living dead.

I believe there is a fear in the church that says if we accept the free grace of God and teach others about it, we will somehow give people the idea that they are free to remain in their sin, that is, separate from God. (That is the risk of a genuine love that allows the freedom of choice and the freedom to walk away.) Why would anyone wish to remain in that void of God and all things good?? God already forgave, but why live as the walking dead for any amount of time and abuse His love and forgiveness in the meantime? Our actions are merely an indication of where our beliefs lie, just as a sore throat is an indication of an underlying sickness. Living in intentional sin reveals that we would rather live apart from God and get what we can for ourselves in our own strength. Falling into bad habits and expressing a nature contrary to God's reveals that there is a wrong belief somewhere that needs to be changed or transfigured through the renewing of our minds.[6] We must trust in the transformational power of God's love, grace, and mercy.

---

6   "Do not be conformed to this world, but be transformed by the renewal of your mind, that by testing you may discern what is the will of God, what is good and acceptable and perfect." (Romans 12:2)

Someone might claim to be a Christian (meaning "little Christ"), but if their life does not look like His, do they really believe it? Someone might say they love you, but if their actions are not loving toward you, do they really love you? We can say we believe anything we say, but our words are only true if they are reflected in our actions. We might even *think* we believe something, but it is what we *do* that reveals what we actually believe. If we intentionally choose to live outside of God's love by choosing our own self-centered gratification and living contrary to what God says is good, it is a sign that we don't really understand what Jesus has done for us, that we don't truly believe and haven't received God's love.

What we do, how we love, and *even our very faith* do not qualify us for inclusion in the New Covenant; Jesus qualifies us. Our belief simply positions us to receive the benefits of His right-standing in the New Covenant. When we truly believe that Jesus made a way for us to be restored to relationship with God, we turn away from the sin that separated us from Him and turn toward Him (repentance). Our actions then follow that belief, and over time, the way we love looks more and more like Him.

But there are many other beliefs we hold on to, and our actions follow *all* our beliefs, not only our belief in Jesus (the belief that positions us for inclusion in Him). Even if we are conflicted in our beliefs, which at times we all are, that does not exclude us from inclusion in God. For example, we might struggle with the belief that we are unworthy of His love. That belief does not change anything about His love or our position in Him. He loves us and we are worthy because He says we are worthy. But we may unconsciously or consciously reject His love and its life-giving, life-changing benefits because of that belief. Your actions, and therefore experiences, will align with that belief. That belief is a lie, and it will hinder you as long as you allow it to have a voice in your life. When we believe a lie it operates like truth in our life, even though it is not truth. Lies have tremendous impact on us in this life, but they will never trump the Truth of God. If you believe in Him, you are in Him, despite any lie that speaks to the contrary.

Fear comes from wrong belief; it is the absence of love, the absence of God. Fear is torment. God does not torment; rather, we torment ourselves (usually unintentionally) through our wrong beliefs. God's love casts out all fear![7] And it is only through His love that our wrong beliefs can truly change.

Many of our beliefs are unconscious. Our beliefs sometimes change only slowly (especially those beliefs we are not aware we hold), and usually only change in time spent with God. And as we surrender those beliefs to Him, He refines them, aligning our beliefs with the Truth, making us more and more like Him in the process, and it is a process. As we spend time with Him and learn the value of giving of oneself and even suffering for the sake of others, like Jesus did, we learn to love the way He did, and it shows in our lives as a marker and a testimony for others to see. I believe this process of learning to love like Jesus

---

7 "So we have come to know and to believe the love that God has for us. God is love, and whoever abides in love abides in God, and God abides in him. By this is love perfected with us, so that we may have confidence for the day of judgment, because as he is so also are we in this world. There is no fear in love, but perfect love casts out fear. For fear has to do with punishment, and whoever fears has not been perfected in love." (1 John 4:16-18)

loved is what Paul was referring to when talking about working out our salvation in Philippians 2:12.[8]

In the New Covenant, self-sacrificial love is an expression of gratitude in response to the gift of the lover of our souls. It is our way of saying, "thank you" to Him. When we begin to truly understand the gift He has given us, the gift of Himself, there can be no other response than to love as He loved.

If you find yourself unintentionally acting in selfish ways apart from God's ways, do not use that as a reason for self-condemnation, but rather use it as an indicator that there is another part of you that needs to be surrendered to God's pruners, a wrong belief that needs to be cut off, burned up, and replaced with God's Truth. We all make mistakes, and we all act habitually according to old habits, but don't stay there! That behavior was the old you, not the new you. Everything happens in the spirit (or unseen) first, and in the physical (or seen) second. Continue to allow the reality of the unseen to manifest in the seen. Sometimes, that takes time! God is not surprised. So don't give up! Surrender once again to Him; He is the great physician, and when we are "sick" with the decay of the world's system, that is precisely when we need Him most. Dive fully into Him! He loves you more than you can even fathom. He is the greatest blessing and gift that has ever been given. But we must lose our old lives in order to find them new in Him.[9]

---

8   "Therefore, my beloved, as you have always obeyed, so now, not only as in my presence but much more in my absence, work out your own salvation with fear and trembling, for it is God who works in you, both to will and to work for his good pleasure." (Philippians 2:12-13)

9   "For whoever would save his life will lose it, but whoever loses his life for my sake will find it." (Matthew 16:25)

CHAPTER 10
WHAT DID I JUST EAT??

So how do we know what tree we have been eating from? What are the signs or symptoms we can look for? Just as the fruit of a physical tree is an identifier of the type of tree that produced it, so does the fruit in our lives reveal which tree we are eating from, which system we are operating under. Keep in mind that different areas of our lives may reflect the fruit of a different tree depending on our current set of beliefs, our maturity, and level of surrender to God.

POSITION VS. PERFORMANCE IN ACTION

I grew up in churches that taught there was nothing I could do to earn my salvation, that salvation from sin and death was a free gift that could only be received, never earned. This is true! However, I was also taught that I must obey the Ten Commandments, pray without ceasing, read my Bible an hour every day, attend church every Sunday, etc., etc., in order to "be a good Christian." All those things are good; however, they are performance-based, and it conveyed the conflicting idea that position with God still needed to be earned even though it could only be received as a free gift. I've known many believers, and was one myself, who lived in constant fear of someday being rejected by God because they didn't do that one thing "just right."

Another problem is that as you go from church to church, denomination to denomination, continent to continent, that list of things you must do in order to be a "good Christian" varies *drastically*. In one church it might be sufficient to generally be a good person (whatever that means) and attend church on Christmas and Easter. Another church might require attendance at 5 or 6 meetings every week, and if you miss one people start questioning your salvation. Another church might require a long pilgrimage on foot every year to prove your devotion to God. But these are all religious acts with the underlying (subtle or blatant) requirement of performance for salvation if the heart of expressing God's love is missing.

Religious acts (for the sake of performance) also put the focus on us and our actions rather than on God, His gifts, and our relationship with Him. Often times, that devotion to religious duty and obligation actually pulls our attention off God and causes us to behave in self-serving ways, causing us to fall back under the system of the Tree of Knowledge and act in ways contrary to who God is, rather than just being brothers of Jesus and allowing that position to shine through us in our self-sacrificial love. It's no wonder that people have been confused and turned off by the religious systems of the church! I think we all have been guilty at times of portraying the Gospel (the good news of what Jesus did for us) according to the wrong system, the wrong tree.

Side note: This is not to say that religious acts are entirely self-serving; often times, traditions and religious rituals, when performed in a heart of devotion and in relationship with God, can be incredibly edifying, helping us remember what God has done for us, enhancing our engagement with Him, and drawing us closer to Him. As with anything we do, we must examine our hearts for the *why* behind our actions. Are we performing out of obligation or to earn something, or are we responding to God's love out of devotion and gratitude?

For you see, even though we do not have access to the physical Trees of Knowledge or Life, we constantly choose which tree we will eat from moment by moment, day by day, and we manifest the fruit of that tree in our hearts and lives and plant the seeds from that fruit through our words and actions. When we choose to put ourselves first for what we can gain for our own good and ignore the needs of others, we choose the fruit of the Tree of Knowledge. Self-serving, self-protection and all-around selfishness grows in us, often at the expense of others, producing death in us and the world around us. When we choose to put the needs of others first and look for ways to serve and love others with our lives (in spite of our own selfish desires), we eat from the Tree of Life, and life is produced in us *and* in others around us.

Again, keep in mind that our self-sacrificial love for others must come from a posture of eyes-always-on-God, in relationship with Him, receiving from Him in order to then give to others, and not from a posture of loving from our own strength or earning position with God! Our actions can *look* self-sacrificial, when in truth they are very much self-serving. A person might give up everything to open an orphanage in Africa, for example, for selfish reasons or for self-sacrificial reasons. The difference between the two is the person's *motive*. *Why* are you starting an orphanage? Is it because you doubt God's love for you, and you think God will love you more if you do something so extreme "for Him?" Or are you opening the orphanage because God moved on your heart and gave you His love for orphans and His desire to go and take care of them? Are you motivated by *fear* (the Tree of Knowledge) or by *love* (the Tree of Life)? Are you *doing to be* or *being to do?*

Too many of us have wasted huge chunks of our lives pursuing projects that God never meant for us to pursue purely because our motives were based not on love and obedience, but on fear. God is good, and He does not allow anything to go to waste; if He turns everything meant for evil to our good,[1] how much more will He use things intended for good for good? But He cannot bless us the way He would like to when we are working out of our own strength, doing works of our own creation; if He were to bless us too richly, we would rightfully believe that we earned those blessings (and they wouldn't be blessings at all, but wages earned). He can only truly bless us when we are acting in obedience to Him, in submission to Him, surrendered to His plans and not our own, and giving to others out of the abundance He gives to us. We must follow in Jesus' footsteps and only do what we see our Father doing.

When we focus on doing, works and achieving, we are focused on the fallen, earth-based system, and we reproduce the fruit of the Tree of Knowledge. Under the system of the Tree of Life, it is about *who,* and *Whose,* we are rather than what we *do*. We can even *try* to be sons[2] of God, but if we are trying, we've missed the point, and we are still focused on achievement and have inadvertently fallen back under the

---

1 "And we know that for those who love God all things work together for good, for those who are called according to his purpose." (Romans 8:28)

2 Being a *son* of God has nothing to do with gender, and everything to do with position and inheritance. Sons know and assist in their father's business, and, according to Hebrew tradition, it is the sons who receive an inheritance in their father's estate.

Tree of Knowledge. If you are *trying* to become something, you are admitting that you are not that thing. We *are* sons of God because that is what God calls us,[3] and for no other reason. When we rest in our identity in Jesus, just *being,* we eat from the Tree of Life, and we then live from that place of abundance, reproducing life in the world around us as we live. What we do, and how we live, then flows from the place of abundance and overflow (life), in rest, rather than striving and struggling from a place of lack (death).

THE ROOT OF FEAR

One of the consequences of the consumption of the Tree of Knowledge is lack, toil and striving to produce.[4] With it comes the constant fear that there might not be enough. Even when the harvest is plentiful in your life, even when you have more than enough, fear prevails because you never know when famine will come. We see the prevalence of the fear of lack even today, even in the wealthiest time period in history. No amount of abundance can ever take away that fear of lack, so we struggle and toil to produce more, to gain a sense of security that can

---

3   "Blessed be the God and Father of our Lord Jesus Christ, who has blessed us in Christ with every spiritual blessing in the heavenly places, even as he chose us in him before the foundation of the world, that we should be holy and blameless before him. In love he predestined us for adoption to himself as sons through Jesus Christ, according to the purpose of his will, to the praise of his glorious grace, with which he has blessed us in the Beloved." (Ephesians 1:3-6)

4   "And to Adam he said, 'Because you have listened to the voice of your wife and have eaten of the tree of which I commanded you, "You shall not eat of it," cursed is the ground because of you; in pain you shall eat of it all the days of your life; thorns and thistles it shall bring forth for you; and you shall eat the plants of the field. By the sweat of your face you shall eat bread, till you return to the ground, for out of it you were taken; for you are dust, and to dust you shall return.'" (Genesis 3:17-19)

never really take away that fear of lack. We think that if we just had a little more (or a lot more), then everything would be ok and we could relax, yet even the wealthiest people in the world can tell you that no matter how much they have, it is never enough.

That fear of lack is ultimately an indicator that we are living from our own means, as an orphan apart from God, not fully trusting in His ability and willingness to provide. We may even feel like that fear is justified because we have experienced real times of lack in our lives, both physically and emotionally. It is our position apart from Him and His abundance that creates a perception of lack in spite of anything we may have been actually given. In reality, the wealthiest person alive is not the one who has everything, but the one who is content with what he has. God may not always give us what we want, but if we choose to trust Him, He will give us everything we need, and if we allow it, He will also shift our desires to match His desires for our lives. The more we learn to trust Him, the more our circumstances will reveal to us that we can trust Him with every aspect of our lives and hearts, until we believe *fully* that we can trust Him completely. This is sometimes a lengthy process, especially if we are intent on holding on to fear and self-preservation, preferring (and ultimately choosing) to believe what we see and experience over what God says and what we might know to be true.

A good friend of mine once told me that all fear is ultimately the fear of death. Fear of people is a fear of social death, fear of losing one's job is a fear of financial death, fear in relationship is a fear of emotional death, and so on. What's more is that fear masquerades as many different forms and expressions, including anger (in most of its forms), jealousy, bitterness, anxiety, depression, impatience, self-protection, defensiveness, aggression, resentment, unforgiveness, stress, etc., all of which boil down to the fear of a death of some kind.

Furthermore, fear (in all its forms) puts the body into a state of fight-or-flight mode in which all unnecessary bodily systems shut down, including even healing. When you are faced with a short-term threat, such as a bear chasing after you, healing (and a number of normal bodily functions) is no longer important. It doesn't matter if you digest your food if you won't be alive in ten minutes. All of your bodily resources are conserved in that moment and redirected toward self-preservation. In the moment of a life-threatening event, these bodily responses are beautifully designed by God to ensure our immediate survival. However, when we live under the constant state of fear (and remember that fear is a byproduct of the fruit of the Tree of Knowledge) we live in a constant state of fight-or-flight, which limits our body's ability to heal, causing eventual physical death in the body. So, the fear of death eventually produces actual death in the body.

ROOTED IN REST

Conversely, when we live in a state of complete rest, trusting in God for all our needs regardless of the appearance of what is going on around us in the world, our bodies can then function fully as designed, at rest and in peak performance. Most Western medicine is designed not to heal directly, but to help us cope with the symptoms of disease, giving our bodies time to heal. When provided with the right nutrients, with healing of the mental and emotional wounds that are causing stress and fear (conscious or unconscious), and with a change in our beliefs as we learn to trust in God (allowing us to enter a state of rest), I believe our bodies are designed to heal just about anything, including even those things we typically associate as a part of the "natural" aging process.[5] When we reside fully under the system (and the person) of the Tree of Life, never subjecting ourselves to fear or death from the system of the Tree of Knowledge, then we enter into the fullness of God's health and life.

If fear that leads to death is the fruit of the Tree of Knowledge, then the fruit of the Tree of Life is faith that leads to life. Faith is a profound belief and trust in God, in what He says is Truth, even if we cannot see or understand it yet, even when the circumstances around us don't seem to match up to what we think we know to be true.[6] Faith produces rest, confidence, and assurance in something greater than and outside of ourselves, something independent from our own strengths and abilities. Faith is necessary on this earth when we are unable to see fully what is going on in other dimensions of the unseen realities around us. Faith is our choice to believe even when what we are believing seems impossible. It is also a gift from God, like a pat on the back from a father encouraging his toddler to walk and not give up when she falls down. Just as fear manifests in a variety of ways, faith also manifests in a variety of different ways, including the presence of love,

---

5   For more information on how fear affects the body's ability to heal, check out *The Love Code* by Alexander Loyd, PhD, ND. Dr. Loyd speaks primarily to unbelievers, and the focus of the book is on the healing power of love. Authentic love by itself is incredibly healing, even to unbelievers, and it is also the highest form of faith, which involves relationship with God, who is the source of all love and ultimate healing.

6   "Now faith is the assurance of things hoped for, the conviction of things not seen." (Hebrews 11:1)

joy, peace, patience, kindness, goodness, gentleness, self-control,[7] etc. Not coincidentally, these are also characteristics of God and byproducts of time spent with Him, in Him.

IDENTIFY THE ROOT, THEN HEAL THE FEAR

Both faith and fear are choices, and both can be planted in the world and people around us by the verbal and non-verbal words we say. They can be passed down from generation to generation. Have you ever wondered why you are absolutely terrified of something that you have never personally experienced? It is likely that one of your ancestors experienced it and passed that fear along to you. Does your family have a history of anger, depression, self-sabotage, violence, addiction, unexplained death, etc.? Remember that all of those things have a root of fear and are manifestations of the fruit of the Tree of Knowledge. Or perhaps you have a family history of faith, of peace, wholeness, love for others, and so many other signs of life. Those kinds of trends become especially obvious in family lines, but they can also be seen in communities, companies, churches, and even in countries. Just as seeds are scattered from field to field both intentionally and unintentionally, the fruit we eat and plant in our own hearts spreads to the hearts of those around us, both intentionally and unintentionally.

---

7   "But the fruit of the Spirit is love, joy, peace, patience, kindness, goodness, faithfulness, gentleness, self-control; against such things there is no law."
(Galatians 5:22-23)

One thing that is of particular importance to note is that both faith and fear are positional, meaning they are places of residence, rather than things we either fight off or muster up. Fear is the fruit of the Tree of Knowledge and faith is a fruit of the Tree of Life; those are two different systems, two different positions, two different places of residence; one is in God, one is outside of God. The system of slavery to the fear of death was established through striving and attempted self-achievement. What makes us think that by trying really hard, we can somehow exit that system of slavery when trying is what got us there in the first place? In other words, we cannot fight fear or achieve faith by eating from the Tree of Knowledge.

Faith and fear are choices, yes, but when we actively engage them through the earth-based system of striving and achievement, we will always fail because we are using the very tools of striving and self that established the fear-based system in the first place. Many well-meaning people have tried to overcome their fears through an active battle of the will; they may have marginal, often temporary success, but the battle remains as a perpetual cycle that they will have to actively engage indefinitely. Residing in fear is not an option unless you wish to submit to death, but fighting fear actually empowers the fear because it keeps you bound in the system of slavery to fear itself.

Fear must be healed, not fought, and you can only begin to heal from fear when you have removed yourself from its system. (As we leave the system of death and fear and enter the system of life, there we find the love that most perfectly heals fear.[8]) If you step in a fire and burn your

8 "There is no fear in love, but perfect love casts out fear. For fear has to do with

92

foot, remaining in the fire will only cause more damage; your foot cannot begin to heal until you step out of the fire. Life and healing can never be found in a system of death and fear.

Likewise, many well-meaning people have tried to muster up enough faith to overcome fear, sickness and death through self-effort and will-power alone. We foolishly believe that striving through our own means and strength can somehow produce life *("If I just try hard enough...")*, when striving and self-achievement are what established us in the system of fear and death in the first place. Rather, we must choose to turn away from fear and toward faith, stepping into life Himself, believing that what God says is Truth, and rest in *His* faith, knowing that it is not our faith, our doing, that brings life, but that He alone is the source of life eternal. When we believe, we position ourselves in Him, in spite of the fact that we still see the results of sin and death all around us in this world, trusting that He will provide according to His promises, trusting that He will always work things out for our good, even *if* His provisions don't seem to match what we think we want and when we want it—that is true faith. No matter the circumstances, no matter the appearance of things, we must abide in Him,[9] because He is the Tree of Life.

REMINDER: *do not be tempted to fall into self-condemnation if you're not there yet and you still struggle with fear, belief, and trust! Self-condemnation keeps us bound under the system of death and separation.*

---

punishment, and whoever fears has not been perfected in love." (1 John 4:18)

9   "I am the vine; you are the branches. Whoever abides in me and I in him, he it is that bears much fruit, for apart from me you can do nothing." (John 15:5)

Don't stay there! Receive His forgiveness, believe He forgives you, abide in His love, and keep going! He hasn't given up on you—don't you give up on yourself!

CHAPTER 11
WHO IS YOUR FATHER?

Another parallel to the idea of fruit trees found throughout Scripture is the idea of familial heritage. Family lineage is of extreme importance throughout the Old and New Testaments. In the Old Testament, the focus is primarily on physical lineage, and in the New Testament we see a shift in focus to spiritual lineage. For example, do you remember Abraham and God's promise to bless his familial descendants?[1] The word God uses for *descendants* in the original Hebrew is the word *zera* (עֶרַ), which means *seed* or *offspring*. Just as the seed of a fruit tree reproduces more of that same fruit tree, so the offspring of a father are like the father. The idea of physical seed and physical lineage are fairly straightforward and easy to understand; spiritual seed and spiritual lineage require a step or more beyond our natural understanding, although the root concepts are similar.

Before the beginning of the creation of the universe, one of God's top-ranking angels, Lucifer, filled with pride, decided that he did not want to submit to God, but rather wanted to be God, to replace the most

---

1   "'This is what the Lord says: Because you have obeyed me and have not withheld even your son, your only son, I swear by my own name that I will certainly bless you. I will multiply your descendants beyond number, like the stars in the sky and the sand on the seashore. Your descendants will conquer the cities of their enemies. And through your descendants all the nations of the earth will be blessed—all because you have obeyed me.'" (Genesis 22:16-18)

high God, and he led a rebellion against God among the angels. The rebellion was unsuccessful, and Lucifer, with a third of all the angels, fell from glory and was removed from God's presence. In the absence of God, they became nothing that He is and everything He is not, and they hated Him even more. Lucifer knew he could never defeat God and replace Him in totality, but he could usurp God's place as the father of the new species of humans who were to be made to be just like God.

So, Lucifer entered God's new creation in the form of a serpent, and he talked to Eve, deceiving her into believing the lie that God didn't really love her and was keeping something good from her, a thing that she could obtain in her own strength if she just disobeyed God and ate the fruit of the Tree of Knowledge. If she took and ate, then she could be just like God, he told her. It was the same lie that Lucifer believed about himself, that he could somehow replace God on his own, in his own strength and power.

Eve bought the lie, Adam followed suit in disobedience, and in their act of rebellion, they hid themselves from God's presence. Outside of His presence, they became everything that God is not and everything that Lucifer had also become in the void of God. Lucifer had become, in a way, the god of the void; now anyone who rejected God by acting unlike Him, in disobedience to Him, not surrendered to Him, would knowingly or unknowingly (in the same motion of rejecting God) be positioning themselves in surrender and obedience to the god of the void. Lucifer could never depose God and usurp His place ultimately, but he was successful in becoming the god and father of humanity, if only for a time. Now, instead of multiplying God's image on Earth as they were created to do, Adam and Eve began to multiply the image of their new father, bringing death and destruction wherever they went.

RIGHTFUL PATERNITY RESTORED

About 2,000 years later, God began His redemption plan for humanity through Abraham, and He offered Abraham a promise to not just bless him with an enormous family, but also to bless his family, and through him, to bless all of humanity. Abraham believed, and it was counted to him as righteousness.[2] Notice something important here: Abraham did not *do* anything, he merely *believed,* and because he believed, he was able to receive the promise and God considered him righteous because of the belief.[3] What is also important to note is that Abraham's actions from that point forward reveal that belief.[4] In other words, Abraham acted as though he believed God would fulfill His promise from that point forward. He received the promise by faith and acted in hope that it would come to pass as God said. God did not act as quickly as Abraham expected, and at one point, Abraham messed up and tried to make things happen through his own strength and means and had a son, Ishmael, by his wife's servant, Haggai. God tells Abraham that Ishmael, while he would be blessed by God, was not the

---

2 "And he believed the Lord, and he counted it to him as righteousness." (Genesis 15:6)

3 "'For if Abraham was justified by works, he has something to boast about, but not before God. For what does the Scripture say? 'Abraham believed God, and it was counted to him as righteousness.' Now to the one who works, his wages are not counted as a gift but as his due. And to the one who does not work but believes in him who justifies the ungodly, his faith is counted as righteousness...'" (Romans 4:2-5)

4 James 2:18-26

fulfillment of His promise. He doesn't abandon Abraham because of his mistake, but through His power and means enables Abraham and Sarah to have the son God promised, Isaac, even though she was barren and well past menopause and Abraham was about 100 years old. Through Isaac was born Jacob, later renamed Israel by God. God chose to bring his promise to Abraham and the world through Israel and his descendants.

Another 2,000 years later, Jesus entered the scene as the Promised One, but He came in a way completely unexpected by the Israelites at the time. They expected a king according to earthly standards, yet Jesus was born in a stable to lowly parents from one of the least-respected cities in the region. His birth was celebrated by some of the lowest in society, shepherds. He grew up apprenticed to His earthly father as a carpenter, not a king, not even a priest. Yet He rose to fame overnight once word of His miraculous healings began to spread. Perhaps this was the Promised One, the Messiah, the Savior of Israel (and of the world)?

Jesus came as one under the Law of Moses and revealed God's true intent for the Law in how He lived and how He taught. He did not honor the traditions of men, and openly taught against empty religious pursuits and practices, which angered the religious leaders tremendously. They heard His words of life and truth, and although a few believed, most of the religious leaders chose instead to hold tightly to the religious traditions (and the power and prestige it afforded them).

God does not take the responsibility of leadership and teaching lightly, because leaders and teachers have the power and responsibility to sway the hearts of the people toward or away from Him. Influence is not something to be taken for granted or treated flippantly. Because of this, Jesus did not mince words when speaking to the religious leaders. He was very kind in dealing with sinners. But with the religious leaders who knew the Law backward and forward and should have known the heart and love of God (yet chose instead to pursue their own gain at the expense of the general population) Jesus had little patience. In one encounter, He says to them:

> "But woe to you, scribes and Pharisees, hypocrites! For you shut the kingdom of heaven in people's faces. For you neither enter yourselves nor allow those who would enter to go in....Woe to you, scribes and Pharisees, hypocrites! For you are like whitewashed tombs, which outwardly appear beautiful, but within are full of dead people's bones and all uncleanness. So you also outwardly appear righteous to others, but within you are full of hypocrisy and lawlessness."
> (Matthew 23:13,27-28)

The religious leaders believed that by merely performing the Law to the letter and by their birthright as sons of Abraham through Israel, they were doing everything right, doing everything they needed to do to make themselves right before God, and that they had earned position with God. They looked down on anyone else who was not flawless in their performance before God. Yet their hearts looked nothing like God's heart.

In another passage, Jesus, knowing their intent to kill Him, talks to some of the religious leaders, confronting them about their unbelief, and slavery to sin and death. They defend themselves by saying, "We are offspring of Abraham and have never been enslaved to anyone,"[5] and "We have one Father—even God!"[6] to which Jesus replies:

> *"If God were your Father, you would love me, for I came from God and I am here. I came not of my own accord, but he sent me. Why do you not understand what I say? It is because you cannot bear to hear my word. You are of your father the devil, and your will is to do your father's desires. He was a murderer from the beginning, and does not stand in the truth, because there is no truth in him. When he lies, he speaks out of his own character, for he is a liar and the father of lies. But because I tell the truth, you do not believe me."* (John 8:42-45)

To the religious leaders, this would have been a *massive* slap in the face, to put it mildly! Being called sons of God and sons of Abraham was at the core of their identity. It was a bragging right, something that they lorded over any gentile, anyone who was not descended from Abraham, through Israel. They looked on Gentiles with utter disdain. Essentially, Jesus was saying the religious leaders had no claim to Abraham as father, and rather were offspring of their father, the devil (Lucifer)!

Jesus is not merely calling people names for the sake of offending them. He is revealing a much deeper truth to the idea of familial lineage. They may have been genetically related to Abraham, but they were not

---

5   John 8:33

6   John 8:41

acting like him. Abraham *believed* and was counted righteous. They refused to believe the truth that Jesus represented, instead choosing to believe lies and trusting in their own works to earn position, revealing that their true father was not God but the devil.

Paul puts it another way:

> "*For not all who are descended from Israel belong to Israel, and not all are children of Abraham because they are his offspring, but 'Through Isaac shall your offspring be named.' This means that it is not the children of the flesh who are the children of God, but the children of the promise are counted as offspring.*" (Romans 9:6b-8)

In other words, what makes a person a child of Abraham, belonging to Israel, is *belief* in the promise given through God's strength and means, not anything accomplished by ourselves or any other person through works. Paul goes on to say that even though the physical descendants of Israel had the Law which should lead a person to righteousness by following the Law through faith and belief, they completely missed the heart of God by pursuing works and good deeds.[7] It was partly because of this mindset they didn't recognize or believe the Promised One when He came.

---

7 "What shall we say, then? That Gentiles who did not pursue righteousness have attained it, that is, a righteousness that is by faith; but that Israel who pursued a law that would lead to righteousness did not succeed in reaching that law. Why? Because they did not pursue it by faith, but as if it were based on works. (Romans 9:30-32a)

ACTIONS REVEAL BELIEFS

So what father are you serving? When we *believe* God's promises that we don't yet see fulfilled, and as a result, live like we believe them (that is faith), then we show that our Father is God and we are His children. When we rely on the works we think are right and good for our justification (even if God also says they are right and good), instead of acting in faith, we show that we are serving the wrong father, and we are attempting to earn what can only be received as a free gift.

This is why just *being a good person* isn't good enough. "Good enough" can never be achieved because at its core it is striving for achievement and self-attainment in the same way that Eve tried to attain God-likeness through her own strength, her own means. "Good enough" is a myth, a lie. No one can be good except God,[8] and goodness can never be earned, only received, through faith.

God *is* love. God's love doesn't come in degrees, it just *is*. No matter how hard you try, no matter how much you do, no matter how badly you've failed, His love for you is still the same. If you try to earn His love, you actually distance yourself from Him. *He* doesn't move; *you* do. There is nothing you can do to *earn* God's love. All you can do is choose to *believe* He loves you and *receive*. And then go and let your life be a reflection of that belief and His love.

As I've heard others say, we need to *be to do,* not *do to be.*

---

8   "And Jesus said to him, "Why do you call me good? No one is good except God alone." (Mark 10:18)

CHAPTER 12
LAW AS DISCIPLINE

By this point in the book, hopefully you have begun to understand the dangers of following law through performance as a means to earn right-standing with God. When we believe in Jesus, we position ourselves *in* Him, and He imparts to us *His* righteousness, *His* right-standing *in* God. It is something that can never be earned, only received. When we try to earn right-standing by works, we position ourselves outside of Him. Under the Old Covenant, a person who followed the Law by faith, trusting in the promise of God and not the works of their hands, received the promises of that covenant. If we (under the New Covenant) try to go back to the Old Covenant and earn position with God through obedience to the Law of Moses, we submit ourselves to the Old Covenant and its terms and conditions,[1] by which we can never be justified before God.[2] Worse than that, we reject the death of Jesus, and state that His blood was not sufficient in that we must also (in or-

---

1   "For all who have sinned without the law will also perish without the law, and all who have sinned under the law will be judged by the law." (Romans 2:12)

2   "For by works of the law no human being will be justified in his sight, since through the law comes knowledge of sin." (Romans 3:20)

"We ourselves are Jews by birth and not Gentile sinners; yet we know that a person is not justified by works of the law but through faith in Jesus Christ, so we also have believed in Christ Jesus, in order to be justified by faith in Christ and not by works of the law, because by works of the law no one will be justified." (Galatians 2:15-16)

der to follow the whole of the Law[3]) return to animal sacrifices for the covering of sin, thereby removing ourselves from the New Covenant established by the blood of Jesus, including the removal of our sins![4]

It is not wrong to abandon the Old Covenant; it is necessary! Paul compares it to a marriage. If a husband were still alive and the wife went to live with another man, then she would be considered an adulteress. But when the husband dies, the wife is free from the law of that marriage to marry another without guilt. She does not dishonor the first marriage by remarrying, but she is free from the law of that marriage.[5] In other words, God, as the husband in the Old Covenant, cannot die, so Jesus (as God and man) died in God's place as well as ours, fully ending the Old Covenant and freeing both parties to establish a New (and far better) Covenant.

We must *never* return to the Law of Moses and the Old Covenant. It was a beautiful gift from God, and much can be learned from it even

---

3   "For whoever keeps the whole law but fails in one point has become guilty of all of it." (James 2:10)

4   "For if I rebuild what I tore down, I prove myself to be a transgressor. For through the law I died to the law, so that I might live to God. I have been crucified with Christ. It is no longer I who live, but Christ who lives in me. And the life I now live in the flesh I live by faith in the Son of God, who loved me and gave himself for me. I do not nullify the grace of God, for if righteousness were through the law, then Christ died for no purpose." (Galatians 2:18-21)

5   "Or do you not know, brothers —for I am speaking to those who know the law— that the law is binding on a person only as long as he lives? For a married woman is bound by law to her husband while he lives, but if her husband dies she is released from the law of marriage. Accordingly, she will be called an adulteress if she lives with another man while her husband is alive. But if her husband dies, she is free from that law, and if she marries another man she is not an adulteress. Likewise, my brothers, you also have died to the law through the body of Christ, so that you may belong to another, to him who has been raised from the dead, in order that we may bear fruit for God." (Romans 7:1-4)

today as all of it points to Jesus, the Kingdom of God, and the New Covenant in some way. It was a tutor and a guide intending to show humanity the need for a savior, but it was never intended to be the end goal:

> *"Now before faith came, we were held captive under the law, imprisoned until the coming faith would be revealed. So then, the law was our guardian until Christ came, in order that we might be justified by faith. But now that faith has come, we are no longer under a guardian, for in Christ Jesus you are all sons of God, through faith."* (Galatians 3:23-26)

I suspect that one of the major reasons why the church has yet to see the fullness of the promises of the New Covenant is due to the fact that, in many ways, we are still operating as though we must be obedient to the Old Covenant, submitting by works and not fully receiving the grace of the New Covenant.

Again, I am not arguing for *lawlessness*. That is very different. Laws are necessary in society because of lawlessness. The New Covenant is not lawless in any way—far from it. As I have mentioned before, the law of the New Covenant is to love as Jesus loved, not as a means to earn position (remember that the New Covenant cannot be broken or upheld by any deed on our part) but as a marker and identifier of one who is included in the Covenant. It is to pour love out in response to the love we have been given. And it is a love that is a higher calling with a greater responsibility and impact than any of the Old Covenantal laws. It is not a lesser calling, but a higher calling. But with it comes tremendous freedom and blessing. Love offers freedom in the removal of endless, tedious codes of conduct, in that there is not just one set response in any situation, but rather love responds with whatever is best in every circumstance, depending on the needs and faith of each person involved. That kind of love requires an intimate relationship with love Himself to know what He would do in each situation.

There are often many occasions in our lives where selfless love *looks* like law, but it can never be done out of a place of works and earning, but truly from a place of genuine care and concern for the wellbeing of others. Think of it more like *discipline* than *law* if that helps. There are seasons in my life where I have had to apply discipline to myself to make sure I go to bed early enough; if I don't and I am under slept, there is a very good chance that I will be impatient and unloving toward my family. My position with God does not change if I go to bed on time or not. However, love for my family compels me to take care of myself so that my own shortcomings (as I learn and grow) do not get the best of me the next day. And even though we are hobby winemakers, and even if I would otherwise enjoy a glass of wine with that meal, as a rule, we do not serve alcohol at certain gatherings in our home because many of the people we minister to struggle with alcohol addiction; but that choice is made out of love, not works.

There is nothing wrong with learning from the Law. It is one of the ways we learn what selfless love looks like. For example, without the Law, we may not realize how harmful and unloving it is to compare ourselves or our possessions to another person.[6] After all, the Law was one of the ways God used to reveal Himself to the world. And every one of us needs discipline as we learn to trust God and grow in faith. Just as it takes time for a child to learn to talk, walk and even eat, it takes time for all of us to grow into maturity as children of God. God is not surprised or offended by your lack of maturity! Would you be angry at an infant for his inability to perform complex mathematical equations? Or fly an airplane? Or even use a toilet and remember to flush? Of course not! That would be absurd, and anyone who did get angry with an infant over things like that would be considered crazy! Yet somehow, we condemn ourselves by assuming that God expects full maturity out of us in our infancy. He knows where we are in our process of maturing better than we do, as well as how to teach us and guide us as we grow. Sometimes, that process requires us to discipline ourselves in a way that looks a little (or a lot) like law. But don't be fooled into trying to earn something; instead, trust God. Administer the same grace to yourself that He gives you when you (like a toddler) stumble and fall as you learn how to walk, then run, and dance.

---

6   "What then shall we say? That the law is sin? By no means! Yet if it had not been for the law, I would not have known sin. For I would not have known what it is to covet if the law had not said, 'You shall not covet.'" (Romans 7:7)

CHAPTER 13
GOD IS NOT IN CONTROL

One thing I have learned over the years that has helped me grow in my understanding and relationship with God more than many other things is the idea that God is not in control, meaning God is not *causing* everything to happen that is happening. He is not *out* of control either, that's not what I'm saying; He is *sovereign* as a king is sovereign over his country. The concept goes hand-in-hand with the idea of free will, the idea that we have a choice as to whether or not to serve and obey Him, to choose Him, or to walk away from Him. God does not want an army of slaves, doing nothing but His bidding, loving Him out of compulsion. He wants family and community, working together *with* Him, not just *for* Him.

We see this dynamic from the very beginning of the Bible in Genesis 1 and 2 where God is working in tandem with other heavenly beings to create the universe and everything in it. John, the apostle, elaborates further on the idea and describes Jesus' role in creation in John 1:1-3: "In the beginning was the Word, and the Word was with God, and the Word was God. He was in the beginning with God. All things were made through him, and without him was not any thing made that was made." It was and always has been a collaboration. And God wants *us* to collaborate with Him as well.

The difficulty with this plan, although essential for the necessity of choice, is that many have chosen not to follow God, but instead pursue their own evil plans and selfish desires. When we pursue our own desires, outside of God, we inevitably do harm to ourselves and especially others. It breaks God's heart to allow it, but the alternative would mean removing freedom of choice and forcing His will on those who have refused Him. As a parent, I can't imagine the pain He must experience watching His children destroy one another and everything good He has given us. He loves us so deeply, yet we repeatedly reject Him and His gifts and choose death and destruction for ourselves and all of creation.

Often times, we attribute the evil in the world to God, as if He planned it and wanted it to happen. The enemy loves it when we do that, because it only increases our desire to distance ourselves from Him. We say, "How could a loving God allow something like this to happen?" But evil is what the people wanted, evil is what the people chose (knowingly or not). He lets us have what we think we want sometimes in hopes that by getting what we wanted apart from Him, including all the negative consequences, we will see the death and destruction for what it is and desire to return to Him. (Think of the story of the Prodigal Son.[1]) Death and destruction were never God's heart or intent! They are merely a natural consequence of separation from Him, who is life and creator.

---

1   Luke 15:11-32

Beyond that, He does not just leave the victims to suffer without help. He works out all things for the ultimate good of those who love Him,[2] including the evil done to us, including the evil we may have done to ourselves. He intervenes in many ways we may not realize, sovereignly, never violating the free will choice of His people, but gently wooing us collectively and individually back to Himself.

When something bad happens, it may be tempting to find comfort in the idea that *God is in control,* especially when everything around us feels so out of control. But I would urge you to look instead to how God is working out your situation for your good. God is not afraid of suffering, and He knows that it can be invaluable for our ultimate good, and for the good of those around us. Ask someone who has come out the other side of tremendous suffering what God has done for them and in them because of it. Not a person would choose to suffer willingly unless they have somehow learned, usually through past suffering, the value it brings to us, not just in this life but in eternity. Paul suffered tremendously as he followed God's leading in spreading the good news of the Gospel throughout the world in his day. This is what he had to say about suffering:

> *"We rejoice in our sufferings, knowing that suffering produces endurance, and endurance produces character, and character produces hope, and hope does not put us to shame, because God's love has been poured into our hearts through the Holy Spirit who has been given to us."* (Romans 5:3b-5)

---

2   "And we know that for those who love God all things work together for good, for those who are called according to his purpose." (Romans 8:28)

If God works out all things for our good, then all things are good to us, even if they do not immediately appear that way in our limited understanding. And we can learn to rejoice in all things, including suffering, because ultimately that suffering perfects us and makes us more like God. Even Jesus was perfected through suffering: "Although he was a son, he learned obedience through what he suffered. And being made perfect, he became the source of eternal salvation to all who obey him..."[3] If Jesus, who was perfect, was somehow perfected through suffering, how much more are we perfected through suffering?

I believe it is suffering that allows us to learn what selfless love is all about. When we are comfortable, we have no reason to think about anyone but ourselves. When we suffer, we learn compassion for others and are given a heart like God's to help those in need, and to change the world for good. Sometimes, that is difficult to see when we are in the midst of the suffering, but give it time and trust God; He knows what He is doing. Even though He is never the source of our suffering, the source of evil, He is faithful and just, He is sovereign over all, and it will work out for good in the end.

---

3   Hebrews 5:8-9

CHAPTER 14
THE CHOICE

Everything in life comes down to one choice, ultimately. That choice manifests in a variety of different ways, but they all boil down to this: will you choose God or reject Him? Based on that choice, we either experience life or death, freedom or slavery, inclusion and family or isolation and separation, abundance or lack, faith or fear, good or evil, love or self. We see this dichotomy everywhere in the world around us. The enemy would like us to believe that there is a gray area between the choices (a middle ground where both choices are really a spectrum), that both can coexist together, or that both choices are equal. We often see the battle between choices play out in others and ourselves, and think it is merely a battle between good and evil. This is true, but the higher reality is that the battle is being waged over *belief* and ultimately *for our hearts*. There is no such thing as *mostly* alive or *mostly* dead; you are either alive or you are dead. You are either a slave or you are free. You either have or you have not. You have either chosen God or you have rejected Him.

We may have a mixture of beliefs and fears that plague us into doubt, such as the fear of whether or not God will accept us. But thankfully, our fears do not change the facts. Our beliefs do not dictate the truth. We tend to see and interpret what we see based on what we believe and who we are, not on how things really are. If we believe the world is a hateful place and everyone is out to get us, we will only see the events that line up with that belief, and beyond that, we will attract more of that kind of attention. If we believe everyone hates us, we will act as though everyone hates us, making our behavior highly unlikeable, and our beliefs become a self-fulfilling prophecy. If we believe that people are generally good and loving, we will act accordingly and will attract good and loving people to ourselves. We experience what we believe and attract more evidence for that belief continually. But just because we believe something doesn't make it true. Thank God! It might seem true to us, it might even be a fact or reality staring us in the face, but what we experience or think we are experiencing will never trump a higher, heavenly reality and what God says is Truth.

That's why the Bible says that faith (the choice to believe what God says is true and acting on that belief) comes about by hearing what God says is true.[1] Often times what God says is the Truth flies in direct opposition to what we perceive and believe, which causes some major internal struggles for most of us! And once again, with every struggle, moment by moment each day, we are faced with the same choice from the beginning: will I choose God and faithful obedience, or will I trust myself and what I see?

Which tree will I eat from today? In this moment?

Thankfully, when we mess up and eat from the Tree of Knowledge, the consequences are nowhere near as detrimental and far-reaching for us (thanks to Jesus!) as they were for Adam and Eve! But if you wonder why you continually see death and destruction in an area of your

---

1 "So faith comes from hearing, and hearing through the word of Christ." (Romans 10:17)

life, examine your heart, then bring your beliefs and your fears before God. Ask Him to show you where the Tree of Knowledge has taken root. Ask Him to show you how to uproot that tree. Submit yourself to His all-consuming fire and allow Him to torch that tree so that it cannot grow back and produce more seed! His fire is painful, but like a splinter being removed, you will feel so much better in the end. Nothing destroys a garden quicker than fire. Also, the smaller the tree, the quicker it will burn; seedlings are especially vulnerable to fire. If the tree is humongous and well-established, it may take longer to burn, but don't give up!

HOW CAN I EAT FROM THE TREE OF LIFE?

When we choose love that prioritizes others, we choose life. Interestingly enough, the opposite of love is not *hate,* although it sometimes plays a part; the opposite of love is *self.* Another way to put it: the absence of love is self, and more specifically, the absence of love is self-centeredness that puts me and my needs first, before others. Ironically, the self-centered absence of genuine love is what the world often calls "love," an idea on which Western culture places inordinate value. It is the very fuel that the abortion industry runs on, sacrificing children on the altar of "my needs come first." A self-centered love brings nothing but death, even in examples that aren't quite as dramatic as abortion. A selfless love goes out of its way to value and uplift others and looks to God for guidance on how to live that out moment by moment.

Ironically, the first step to loving others is to *receive* love for yourself from God and from yourself (notice I did not say *earn*). So, don't try to skip that part. This is *very* different from self-centeredness, often called "self-love," which is only a pride-filled self-glorification. I am referring to allowing the love of God to permeate every aspect of your being, and then loving yourself with the love you receive from Him. With that love comes full and complete grace and acceptance. We must learn to allow God to love us, even when we don't feel worthy, and especially then. Self-hatred is not humility, it is pride; self-hatred is self-glorification mixed with self-condemnation. We must learn to let go of the pride of self-condemnation. If we do find fault upon self-examination, we must learn to surrender that part of ourselves to God and allow Him to change that in us, as that fault is simply a micro-void of Himself, needing to be filled with a remedy that only He can provide. We can work hard at "fixing" ourselves, but then we fall into works apart from Him, and being apart from Him was what caused the problem in the first place. If you boil it down far enough, any problem within ourselves simply reveals a void of His love, and that void can never be filled and healed by anything other than His love. So, we *must* receive His love if we want to be whole, and we must stop pulling away and condemning ourselves, which means we must learn to have grace for ourselves!

Often, we need to take care of ourselves in order to take care of others. That doesn't mean abandoning your family for months while you wander in a foreign country to "find yourself." If we follow Jesus' example, He often withdrew from the crowds of needy people to spend alone time with God. Did He ever have hobbies He liked to pursue? Perhaps, however, most of what we know of His life was from the three years He was involved in intense, God-ordained ministry work, during which He probably did not have a lot of extra time for hobbies. (Most people throughout most of history have not had the time we do today for things like hobbies, downtime, and entertainment. Free time, never mind "me time," is a very new concept.) But Jesus always took time alone to be with God. God *has* to be our priority; He *must* be our source, otherwise we fall into a well-meaning trap of striving to love out of our own strength and means, which eventually leads to physical and/or emotional burnout (a type of death). We must learn to allow His strength, His love, His grace to flow through us in everything we do, but it's difficult to know how to do that unless we are in constant communication with Him. This doesn't mean chattering away constantly at God; we must also listen. Often, it just looks like a continual mindfulness of His presence, which takes practice. And when we do find ourselves in a busy season without much quiet time, as mothers of young children know well, often it is the awareness of His presence while we are elbow-deep in dirty dishes and laundry that sustains us. It is about living intentionally from Him as our source, even if a certain season of care for others doesn't allow the quantity of quiet time we would like. We need to absolutely make it a priority to carve out quiet time with Him, *especially* in those seasons of intense demand!

WHAT TREES AM I PLANTING?

Everything we do and everything we say plants a seed. We constantly choose which tree we plant. Most of us think of words as being harmless, innocuous, but we must remember that it was through the Word

(Jesus), who spoke many words,[2] that the universe and everything in it was created. *What are you creating or destroying with your words?* James said, "So also the tongue is a small member, yet it boasts of great things. How great a forest is set ablaze by such a small fire!"[3] And in the Proverbs, "Death and life are in the power of the tongue, and those who love it will eat its fruits."[4] Not only are we planting words as seeds for the benefit or detriment of others, but we also plant those seeds in our own hearts and minds. What have you been telling yourself and others? Is it the Truth or a lie? And don't forget that our actions speak louder than our words. We can say anything we want, but it is what we do that reveals what we believe, and each belief is rooted in one of two trees.

And above all things, choose life. He loves you dearly. He gave up His Son to death for your sake. Death couldn't hold Him because there was not a hint of anything death-like in Him, so He took the keys of Death and Hades, and is alive forevermore![5] Now He is offering you that same gift, that anything death-like in you be completely buried, washed away, permanently forgiven, so that death can have no hold on you as well! God is the greatest inheritance we could ever be given because He is life and love and peace forevermore. He accepts you fully

---

2   "In the beginning was the Word, and the Word was with God, and the Word was God. He was in the beginning with God. All things were made through him, and without him was not any thing made that was made." (John 1:1-3)

3   James 3:5

4   Proverbs 18:21a

5   "When I saw him, I fell at his feet as though dead. But he laid his right hand on me, saying, 'Fear not, I am the first and the last, and the living one. I died, and behold I am alive forevermore, and I have the keys of Death and Hades.'" (Revelation 1:17-18)

and has waited eagerly for your return to Him as His long-lost child.[6]

Don't keep Him waiting any longer!

---

6   Luke 15:11-32

TREE OF KNOWLEDGE   VS.   TREE OF LIFE

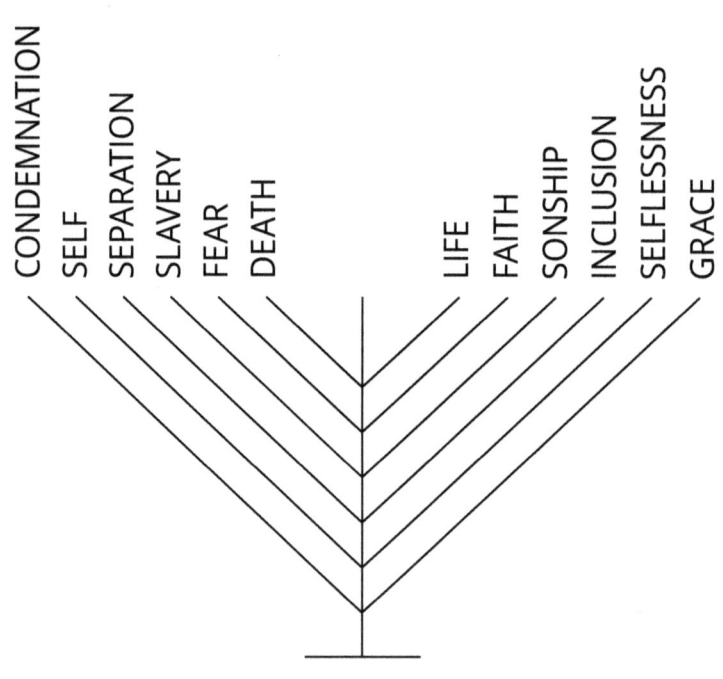

A PRAYER, ESPECIALLY FOR YOU

God,

Make me Yours again. I am sorry I tried to do things on my own, without You. I am sorry I ran away from You and chose other things instead of You. I turn my back on those things, I die to those things today and return to You. I receive the gift of Jesus' blood that washes me clean of all sin and death, and I join Him in His death to my old self and I join Him in His resurrection into His new life. I receive Your love into all the broken places. My life is no longer mine, but Yours. I decree that I am now a brand-new creation in You, nothing like the old, and I invite Your Spirit to come into me, to help me and guide me forever.

Amen

SPECIAL THANKS TO

Evan Doukas

Nancy Wylie

Lisa Guest

Joyce Pettit

Sharon Burns

Jonathan Welton

Chris Blackeby

Kirby de Lanerolle

Justin Abraham

Bill Johnson

The Seraph Creative Team

ABOUT THE AUTHOR

Kirsten Doukas is a daughter, wife, and mother to two beautiful girls. She is a teacher who is actively involved in homeschooling and ministry, as well as a talented graphic and website designer and artist. Together with her husband, Evan, Kirsten is passionate about helping others grow in their love for the Lord and discover their true identity in Him, finding freedom from the bondage of death and decay.

Their shared vision is to see the body of Christ restored to unity and love, embracing the simplicity, goodness, and truth of the happy gospel.

ABOUT THE AUTHOR

Seraph Creative is a collective of artists, writers, theologians & illustrators who desire to see the body of Christ grow into full maturity, walking in their inheritance as Sons Of God on the Earth.

Sign up to our newsletter to know about upcoming releases from this author, as well as other exciting releases.

Visit our website: www.seraphcreative.org

www.ingramcontent.com/pod-product-compliance
Lightning Source LLC
Chambersburg PA
CBHW051214120626
46547CB00013B/1355